Praise for *The Way of the Wilderness Warrior*

Are you ready to undertake the epic journ that hardly exists on any map, to a locati nowhere? Think twice before you set out: of the wilderness, both physical and spiritual, could prove to have far reaching consequences. These pages, written by Dwight Longenecker, will, in any case, prepare you for spiritual battle, for a battle against the world, the devil, and the flesh, not to mention that other terrible adversary: one's own self.

—Dom Philip Anderson
Abbot, Clear Creek Monastery

There are things we read in theology books that sound highfalutin and complicated, things such as concupiscence, poverty, the deadly sins, and mortification. Perhaps the best way to grasp what the Catholic tradition actually reveals by these terms is through a simple story about a simple student who meets a simple hermit. Is Fr. Aelred an eccentric or an ecstatic? Either way, he is out of the center in which most of us live, and from that vantage point, he can shed light on our lives in the world—which is exactly the illumination that monasticism is supposed to shed.

In *The Pilgrim's Regress*, C. S. Lewis has the hermit tell the pilgrim, "You may be sure the Landlord has brought you the shortest way: though I confess it would look an odd journey on a map." In this insightful and edifying book, Fr. Longenecker has the reader join Austin on his odd journey to the hermitage of an imaginary Benedictine monastery, and although the world will think it looks odd, it turns out to be the shortest way, for both him and for ourselves, to the way, the truth, and the life of the world.

—David W. Fagerberg
Professor Emeritus of the Department of Theology,
University of Notre Dame

Like the characters in Fr. Dwight Longenecker's book, we are all on a mission: to become like Christ. Like his characters and like the saints before us, we will travel many different routes, aspiring to arrive at a common destination. In *The Way of the Wilderness Warrior*, Fr. Longenecker speaks with the voice of Austin Fairfax, a college student who, with his friends, embarks upon a very personal journey toward his final destiny.

Fr. Longenecker's broad experience; his knowledge of literature, history, and culture; and his sharp wit and command of the English language color Austin's story. It's a lesson we all need to ponder, delivered in a way that we'll all enjoy.

—Kathy Schiffer
Correspondent and Blogger,
National Catholic Register and *Seasons of Grace*

The Way of the Wilderness Warrior (I've been calling it WWIII) is a Pilgrim's Progress for the twenty-first century. At once deeply theological and brilliantly entertaining, the story takes us on a spiritual odyssey from the depths of a soul's dark night to the heights of consolation, while somehow mysteriously keeping its sense of humor. Fr. Lawrence is an earthy, believable, and charmingly fallible priest; Shelby is as gritty and beautiful as she is wise; and Austin is a thoroughly relatable everyman. Moreover, Fr. Longenecker doesn't pull any punches—and I almost mean that literally. His characters are tough and real. His understanding of human psychology is as deep as his theology, and his prose is hard-hitting—as entertaining as a boxing match, but good for your soul.

—Fr. Augustine Wetta
Author, *The Eighth Arrow* and *Humility Rules*

Having first deftly exposed in his captivating works *Immortal Combat* and *Beheading Hydra* the stark reality of today's intensifying spiritual battle, taking us from the depths of our wounded human nature to the dark forces driving current movements in society and culture, Fr. Dwight Longenecker now gives us the solution: *The Way of the Wilderness Warrior*. And what is the Way? God's call to holiness: we must become saints, especially in these critical times. Jesus' timeless words ring louder than ever: "Be perfect, as your heavenly Father is perfect." Filled with rich, timeless truths of the Faith, Fr. Longenecker shows us the Way, with God's light permeating this compelling work. May we all have the grace to become Wilderness Warriors.

—Norbertine Canonesses of the Bethlehem Priory of St. Joseph,
a cloistered community of Roman Catholic nuns

The Way of the Wilderness Warrior

Also by Dwight Longenecker:

Immortal Combat

An Answer, Not an Argument

Our Lady? A Catholic/Evangelical Debate

St. Benedict and St. Thérèse: The Little Rule and The Little Way

The Secret of the Bethlehem Shepherds

Listen My Son: St. Benedict for Fathers

The Gargoyle Code

Beheading Hydra

Slubgrip Instructs

Catholicism Pure and Simple

More Christianity

The Mystery of the Magi

The Secret of the Bethlehem Shepherds

Praying the Rosary for Inner Healing

Praying the Rosary for Spiritual Warfare

A Sudden Certainty

The Quest for the Creed

The Romance of Religion

Letters on Liturgy

There and Back Again: A Somewhat Religious Odyssey

FR. DWIGHT LONGENECKER

THE WAY OF THE WILDERNESS WARRIOR

SOPHIA INSTITUTE PRESS

Manchester, New Hampshire

Sophia Institute Press

Box 5284, Manchester, NH 03108

1-800-888-9344

www.SophiaInstitute.com

Sophia Institute Press® is a registered trademark of Sophia Institute.

paperback ISBN 978-1-64413-415-3

ebook ISBN 978-1-64413-416-0

Library of Congress Control Number: 2022946356

First printing

To my extraordinary children:
Benedict, Madeleine, Theodore, and Elias

The hero ventures forth from a world of common day into a region of supernatural wonder: fabulous forces are there encountered, and a decisive victory is won. The hero comes back from this mysterious adventure with the power to bestow boons on his fellow man.

–Joseph Campbell

Contents

Acknowledgments

I am grateful to my friends at Belmont Abbey in North Carolina, Quarr Abbey on the Isle of Wight, the abbot and monks of Clear Creek Abbey, and the monks of Norcia, Italy, for their example, welcome, and sanity. Thanks are also due to the Dominicans of St. Stephen's Monastery in Jerusalem and the Norbertine Canonesses at Bethlehem Priory in California for their hospitality, friendship, and support.

The Rule of St Benedict has been a powerful inspiration and guide in my life for many years, and I was first introduced to the way of St. Benedict by June Reynolds—a Benedictine oblate I met when I was a college student. This book is dedicated to my four children but written in honor of June Reynolds—a very ordinary person who followed the Lord Jesus in the path of St. Benedict and whose life I believe, was "hid with Christ in God."

In addition, I wish to thank Professor David Fagerberg; Dom Augustine Wetta, O.S.B.; and Dom Luke Bell, O.S.B., for reading the manuscript and offering suggestions and comments. Thanks, too, to Charlie McKinney and his team at Sophia Institute Press for their encouragement, professionalism, and enthusiasm.

Finally, I thank my parishioners at Our Lady of the Rosary Church in Greenville for being patient with a priest who is also a writer, and for my wife, Alison, and our four children, who astonish me every day with their beauty, intelligence, common sense, and love.

The Way of the Wilderness Warrior

Introduction

As the clown longs to play Hamlet, so I have wanted to write a book on spirituality. However, there are several innate problems in such an enterprise.

First, I am aware that it is easier to read a book about prayer than it is to pray. If the book is inspiring, we might even mistake the inspiration we feel for progress in praying. This would be the same as believing oneself to be well on the way to becoming a concert pianist after being stirred by Rachmaninoff's Third Piano Concerto.

Second, it is not that much harder to *write* a book about prayer than it is to read one. The danger, however, is greater; in writing a book on such a subject, one might come to believe that mastery of theoretical content equates to mastery of the actual spiritual life.

This brings me to the third problem. To write any book, one ought to be an expert; to write a book on spirituality, one therefore ought to be a saint. Alas, I am no John of the Cross, Francis de Sales, or Teresa of Ávila. When it comes to prayer, I feel like a dabbler, a dancer with a clubfoot, a fraud, and a pretender. If a poetaster is a mediocre poet, then I am a "prayertaster." I hesitate to write on spirituality lest anyone imagine that I know what I am talking about at any level above the theoretical.

Then there is the technical problem of writing such a book. If one steps away from giving forthright didactic instruction out of a true awareness of one's unworthiness, one is left with the task of relating the content in some other manner. Instead of being the teacher firsthand, one relies on the words of the great masters themselves. This is the tack taken by David Fagerberg, by Brant Pitre, by Ralph Martin, and by Thomas Merton in his collection of sayings of the Desert Fathers. This seemed apt but somewhat pedantic.

Furthermore, all these attempts at teaching the principles of spirituality tend toward a "method," a plan, a structure that can too often be prescriptive rather than descriptive. This, in turn, can lead to a rigid structure that must be followed—even a legalistic approach. It can turn what is essentially a subjective experience into a mandatory discipline.

These difficulties kept me from making any progress on the book for some months until I happened on the solution. In reading *The Conferences of John Cassian*, I saw that he cracked it. He did not write about the spiritual life as if he were an expert (although I'm sure he was). Instead, he framed his spiritual wisdom in the context of a group of seekers visiting the monks in the Egyptian desert in the fourth century. "Aha!" I said to myself. "He doesn't give the spiritual advice. He puts it into the mouth of a wise old monk." I am not a scholar of monastic literature, so I don't know whether Cassian was quoting the Desert Fathers he met or whether he used a fictional framework to impart his own learning.

My research showed that St. Aelred of Rievaulx did the same in his famous treatise on friendship. St. Gregory also used the device in his dialogues; this tradition of communicating wisdom through a recorded conversation with a sage goes as far back as Socrates and Plato. This dialogue format lets the spiritual master deliver the teaching while engaging the reader in a quest for knowledge.

One problem remained. Most modern readers are not acquainted with an extended dialogue. Therefore, in this book, the dialogue is contained within the framework of a fictional story. I have attempted to write not a fully creative novella but instead a spirituality lesson delivered in the context of a story. It is possible that the attempt fails both as a book on spirituality and as a work of fiction, but I hope this hybrid will appeal to many readers who are willing to overlook its faults and find within it some nuggets of worth.

After I left the Anglican ministry to join the Catholic Church, I had to retrain for a new career. So, somewhat naïvely (but enthusiastically), I took some classes in the craft of script writing for films. Studying the structure of stories led me to the work of the mythologist Joseph Campbell. Campbell's famous work *The Hero with a Thousand Faces* chronicles the similarities among the legends and myths of many cultures. From his lifelong study of myth, Campbell proposed that there was "one story to rule them all"—the story of the hero's quest.

Put very simply, the hero leaves the comfort of his ordinary world and crosses the threshold into a realm of adventure. There he finds the great treasure, defeats his nemesis, wins the fair maiden, and returns home to save those he left behind. Most important, through the great quest, the hero undergoes a transformation. It is the quest itself that makes the hero, as much as the hero that makes the quest. Campbell traces the pattern of this story through all the great tales of humanity, including the great sagas of salvation in the Old Testament. He would have asserted that the same pattern can be discerned in the lives of the apostles and all the great saints of the Church.

The hero's quest therefore provides a kind of template in which the classic insights of the spiritual quest can be filtered and organized. Drawing these ideas together provides the basis for *The Way of the Wilderness Warrior*—the story of one young man's spiritual quest.

Austin Fairfax is a fictional college student who, with some friends, is challenged to learn more about the way to become a saint. As the story develops, he meets a monk who mentors and guides him in his search.

It is my hope that this book will help those who are looking for an accessible and even entertaining way to learn more about Catholic spirituality. In gathering the content for it, I have drawn on Carmelite and Benedictine spirituality as well as classic Catholic teachings on the life of grace.

I remember a Franciscan friar explaining to a group of high school students, "I follow the Lord Jesus Christ in the path of St. Francis." This has always seemed to me a particularly simple and elegant way of describing what it means to be a Catholic Christian. We follow the Lord Jesus Christ, but because the Catholic Faith is so wide and deep, most of us find a path within the Catholic Church that aligns with us as individuals. This helps us to narrow our search, to refine our discipline according to a rule especially suited to our particular circumstances and character, and, ultimately, to deepen our love of Christ. My own way is to follow the Lord Jesus Christ in the path of St. Benedict. Others will follow in the path of St. Thérèse, St. Francis de Sales, St. Ignatius of Loyola, St. Dominic, St. Norbert, St. Teresa of Ávila, or any number of other saints or spiritual writers. My own preference for the Way of St. Benedict should not be understood as a criticism of the other paths. To each his own.

Contemporary Christians often imagine that the sole aim of the Christian life is simply to make it to Heaven. The New Testament scholar N. T. Wright, in his biography of St. Paul, asserts that the early Church's understanding of salvation had much more to do with our transformation in this life. Cooperating with God's grace for our souls' salvation did not simply mean going to Heaven when we die. It meant divinization—being transformed by the power of the Holy Spirit into complete sons and daughters of God and, therefore, brothers and sisters of Christ: to "attain to ... mature manhood, to the extent of the full stature of Christ," as St. Paul puts it in Ephesians (4:13). This is the object of the spiritual life: not just shooting for the stars, but becoming a star; not just being a good person, but becoming a person who is good through and through; not just following Christ, but getting to the point where we are one with Him—where Christ lives in us and we live in Christ, so that we are so much one with Christ that we become unique icons of Him in this world.

That such a transformation is possible is proven by the lives of the saints, and in my experience, there are far more ordinary, down-to-earth, grace-filled Christian disciples who have achieved this than most people realize. We find it hard to believe that such miracles have taken place is because we are distracted both by wicked people and by our own blindness—and also because those who are truly transformed into unique icons of Christ are humble and do not stand out from the crowd. Like all of the saints, their "life is hidden with Christ in God" (Col. 3:3). I hope this book might help to create more of them.

Fr. Dwight Longenecker
Greenville, South Carolina
March 21, 2022
Feast of the Death of St. Benedict

1

Father Lawrence

I met Father Lawrence Roper the first semester of my senior year at the College of Charleston. I had been brought up in a working-class Catholic home and went to Catholic grade school. My dad was proud that I got into college but thought it was useless for me to major in philosophy. Mom nagged me to go to Mass every week, so I started off by dragging myself either to the college chaplaincy or to St. Anthony's, around the corner from the apartment I was sharing with three other guys. It was duty. That's all.

But then we got a new roommate—Charlie Watkins. Charlie had converted to Catholicism from Evangelical Christianity. He was the first person I had ever met who had done that. More often I had heard about Catholics who left the Faith to attend one of those churches that met in what used to be a supermarket. You know—the kind that have Bible studies every other night and on Sundays have praise-and-worship sessions with big screens, a rock band, and some young preacher with skinny jeans and a Starbucks coffee who thinks he's doing a TED talk.

Charlie said he got fed up with all the emotion and hype in the supermarket church. It seemed more like entertainment than religion, he said. So he found the Catholic Church, and every Sunday he'd take an Uber to St. Monica's—Father Roper's parish in North Charleston. Father Roper had a bit of a reputation as a kind of Clint Eastwood character—gritty, but with a tender heart.

The area around St. Monica's Church was pretty rough. Most people know of Charleston, South Carolina, as one of the most beautiful cities in America—and they're right. But it's also one of the neediest cities in America. North Charleston has a big share of the usual urban problems: poverty, homelessness, crime, gangs, drug abuse, human trafficking—you name it.

Father Lawrence was assigned there after he got into some trouble in the Diocese of Dorchester in Baltimore. When I met him, he was in his late sixties; it was after his arrival that St. Monica's started to gain a reputation among the Catholic students at my college. The neighborhood might be crummy, but, by all accounts, the church and the liturgy were splendid.

St. Monica's was one of those old churches that was pretty run-down and shabby, but Father Lawrence begged, borrowed, and maybe stole some old statues and a gothic altarpiece from a church that had been closed. He got some of the local kids to join the choir and convinced one of the music professors from the College of Charleston to volunteer as a music director. Those choristers sang all the classical sacred music, and the college students came flocking to learn it. Somehow or other, Father Lawrence found the money to fix up the old pipe organ, and there were always some music students willing to play it for Mass.

The cadets from the Citadel loved him and used to call him Padre Santini. They're all in love with the Great Santini, that gritty character from the Pat Conroy novel.

Father Lawrence was a good preacher. He didn't cut any corners, and he presented the Faith with a certain amount of blood and thunder. But his parishioners and penitents would smile and agree that he was a lion in the pulpit and a lamb in the confessional. And, whatever he did, it was working. South Carolina is Baptist country, but Father Lawrence was making Catholics out of the Baptist students at an amazing rate, and these converts brought their enthusiasm and Bible knowledge to the Catholic Church, giving Father Lawrence's parish an energy I had not experienced in a Catholic church before.

Eventually, I ended up joining Charlie and the others not only in going to Mass but also as part of the St. Vincent de Paul Society. We worked at boosting the struggling efforts to maintain a food pantry and a soup kitchen, and we raised the money for Father Lawrence's pet project—the Fresh Start Center, where homeless people could drop in, spend the day, establish a postal address by renting a post office box, have a shower, do their laundry, and have a hot lunch. Father Lawrence was there most days, listening to their problems and connecting them with other charities in town.

The first time I met him was over a bowl of soup at Fresh Start, at the end of my first semester. At that point, I had volunteered to help with the hot lunches two days a week.

"What's your name, kid?" he asked.

"Austin."

"Austin what?"

"Austin Fairfax."

"Fairfax. I like that. What does your last name mean?

"I think it's an old English name that means 'blond-haired.' "

"You could change the second 'F' to a 'P,' and it's French for "make peace." Is that your vocation? To be a peacemaker?"

"Nah. I doubt it. It's just a name."

"Did you know the famous .45 Colt revolver was called 'the Peacemaker' in the Old West?"

"Yeah. I'd heard that," I grinned. Didn't I tell you he was a Clint Eastwood kind of guy? For all I knew, he was packing a .45 under his cassock.

"How did you get that first name?" Father asked and, without waiting for an answer, went on, "Do you realize Austin is a short form of Augustine?"

"No. I didn't know that. I'm kind of embarrassed about my name, to tell the truth."

"Why's that?"

"My people are what some folks at Charleston would call 'trailer trash.'"

He frowned, then gave his trademark crooked grin. "Sounds like my kind of people."

"My Dad's from Texas, and he named all of us kids after Texas towns. I'm Austin. I have a brother Dallas and another brother Houston."

Father Lawrence laughed. "Any sisters?"

"Yep. Antonia and Angela. Twins."

"For San Antonio and ...?

"There's a town called San Angelo," I said into my soup.

"Well I think that's sweet," said Father Lawrence. "But maybe you're meant to be Augustine because here you are at St. Monica's. Did you know St. Monica is the mother of St. Augustine?"

"I didn't know that." I grinned. "So this is my mother church?"

"You got it, kid." He slapped me on the shoulder.

And with that he was off to sit at another table with a homeless guy—long hair and scruffy beard, a Gulf War vet.

The next conversation I had with Father Lawrence was in the confessional. To tell you the truth, I was deep into porn in those days, and he told me flat-out that porn was a carcinogen for the soul. It would cause soul cancer—and like most cancers, once it gets going, it's hard to stop. He asked what I was going to do about it and suggested that I join a weekly men's group in which the guys were learning techniques to overcome addictions.

So I started going to the group, which met in his rectory on Wednesday nights after the six o'clock Mass. My roommate Charlie went too, worried as he was about his beer intake. Father Lawrence's housekeeper was an old Italian woman named Flo. She fed us a different kind of pasta every week, and she kept Italian opera blaring from the speakers in the kitchen. Even with the kitchen door closed, once our talks began, we could always hear the crescendos.

Father Lawrence had this theory that practically everybody has some kind of addiction. He said addictions are just shortcuts to happiness in some way, but they are all lies. They promise a quick happiness hit, but they all eventually lead to disaster. Drugs and booze are the obvious examples, but he said that weed, tobacco, and junk food could also do the trick. He explained how every addiction gives you a kick—a high of some kind—and that you keep going back for more of that same feeling, but that every time, you need a little bit more of whatever it is to get the same high.

Then he said something that really blew me away. He said practically everybody has an addiction, but most people are addicted to stuff that society approves of: money, success, entertainment, self-esteem, or sex. All of these, he said, are false pathways to what seems like happiness, but they end up leading to destruction.

We were all supposed to check what our addictions were. I knew mine: the need to succeed in life and the need to break out of my trailer-trash background—and also lurking there was my porn use. Was I addicted to porn? I wasn't sure, but I knew that my porn use was not going in a good direction.

Father Lawrence was running a six-week course. During our last class, he explained that there was only one thing that could bring us the happiness we were all looking for. "There's this bishop in the early Church," he said, "whose name was Augustine." He looked straight at me and nodded.

"Augustine said, 'Our hearts are restless till they find rest in Thee'—in God. It's only in God that the desire that drives us into addictions can really be satisfied. And here's the amazing thing: We don't find our 'rest in God' in some kind of spiritual hammock. We find it on a mountaintop—after going on a long journey toward perfection. This perfection is called union with God. We rest in God only when we are truly united with God in a state of spiritual union."

At this point, my friend Charlie spoke up. "I'm sorry, Father Lawrence, but what are you talking about? Union with God? Perfection? That's impossible!"

He was silent and thoughtful for what felt like ages, but then he finally replied, "Difficult, but not impossible. With God, all things are possible."

Charlie objected, "But nobody's perfect! The Bible says, 'All have sinned and are deprived of the glory of God'" (Rom. 3:23).

Leave it to Charlie always to have a Bible verse handy!

"The Bible also says that we are to 'grow up into the full stature of Christ' and that 'Christ is to be in us and us in Him' and that we are 'sharers in the divine nature' [see Eph. 4:13; 1 John 4:13; 2 Pet. 1:4]. What do you think all that means?"

Charlie shrugged. "I guess I never heard those verses before."

"We are all sinners, but we can be perfected," Father Lawrence went on. "We can be purified. God does this work, but we cooperate with His providence, and I believe our final perfection is better than the perfection that God first made in Adam and Eve."

Charlie frowned. "I don't get it."

"Our second perfection is better because—as individuals and as a human race—we will have entered into sin and death and come through on the other side. Christ enables us to do this, and because He went through death and the great darkness, we can go on that path too. He is the forerunner and the guide. He opens the door, and we can go through it; having gone through the death and darkness, we are triumphant over it. The warrior who has won a victory is a greater warrior than the one who has never fought a battle."

"One of my favorite saints," Father Lawrence continued, "is a bishop from the second century, Irenaeus. He says something like 'God became man in order to unite man with Himself and make him, by adoption, a son of God. God became man so men could become gods.'"

Charlie shook his head, "That's insane—and isn't it like some kind of heresy that you think you can become a god?"

Father Lawrence was shocked. "No! No! Don't misunderstand me! I am not saying I have achieved this. I'm far from it, but I believe I have met a few people who *have* reached that point. But here's the trick: if they have, then they are truly humble people and they would never tell you that they have reached that point. In fact, if you meet someone who *does* believe he has reached the point of perfect purification, he's almost certainly bogus."

His words lit a fire in me. I had never heard anything like it. If what he was saying was true, then it was the most important thing I had ever heard. It was a great treasure, and suddenly I remembered those stories about a woman looking for a lost coin and a father looking for a runaway son.

Then, as if he were reading my mind, he said, "We often think religion is just about getting to Heaven one day and avoiding Hell. That's not religion. That's a fire-insurance policy. What if the point of our religion is not only to get to Heaven but to be brought to a state of union with God—with perfection here in this life? What if this is exactly what you are called to do, what you were created for?"

That Wednesday night, the last before our Christmas break, I made a decision that, looking back on it, I sometimes wish I hadn't made. It was a decision that took me deeper down the rabbit hole than I ever could have known.

2

The Homeless

At the end of that Wednesday-night session, everybody was hanging around, sipping coffee, gorging on Krispy Kreme donuts, and laughing and talking. As usual, I was standing on my own, feeling a bit depressed and in a general bad mood. Father Lawrence came over.

"Austin."

"Yeah?"

"You were especially tuned in there tonight, weren't you?

"I guess."

"But you don't say much."

I smiled. I could tell he understood. "Maybe I'm an introvert."

"Does that bother you?"

"Not really. I just don't fit in. I'm not interested in the stuff most people care about."

"What are you interested in?"

"Philosophy—and what you were talking about."

"Do you like books? Stories? Movies?"

"Sure."

"You know that our course is over, but I want you to know, when you all come back from Christmas, I'm starting a new session—just a short one. Three weeks to take things a bit further. Do you want to join?"

"What's the point?"

"A few of the guys in the addiction class have asked me to teach them more about the path to perfection. Some other folks are interested too. I thought maybe you'd want to take it to the next level."

"Sure," I shrugged.

Father Lawrence frowned. "Don't just give me that little shrug, Austin. Do you want to join in or not?"

Then I really messed up. I rolled my eyes and said, "Whatever."

I could tell that made him mad, but he kept a lid on it. "What if I told you that you really need to be there and that it's a matter of life or death? Would you come?"

"Yes. I'll come."

"A hundred percent sure?"

"A hundred percent," I said.

So the first Wednesday in January, I found my way to the drafty fellowship hall at St. Monica's, not knowing what I was in for. There were nine of us. My friend Charlie came back too, and I spotted Michael—skinny, handsome, with a shock of dark hair. He was another philosophy student. There were also three girls from the soup-kitchen volunteer crew joining us this time—Catherine, Shelby, and Jenny—and I noticed that they looked a little dubious, but maybe they were just shy or uncomfortable. Catherine was slim, with a cute, turned-up nose and a short haircut. Jenny, with a full figure, had a habit of flipping back her shoulder-length hair. Shelby was tall and thin and had a nose ring and an intelligent glint in her eye. I recognized another one of the guys there: JohnMark was a bit pudgy, outgoing, and fun, and he was a regular at the Newman Center. Everybody figured he'd end up in the seminary. I was surprised to see the last two guys who came in. Jordan and Clarke liked hanging around the Newman Center now and again, but breweries and parties were their regular scene. Jordan had put on more than his freshman fifteen, and Clarke—handsome, blond surfer and mountain biker—was always bragging about how much money he was making on the stock market.

Father Lawrence started the session with a short prayer and then jumped right into discussing what he wanted to cover in our class.

"This course is about the spiritual life. It's about a journey and a battle. Everybody is looking for home, but you have to fight to find it. It is a journey because God calls us when we are where we don't belong—we have to figure out how to get from here, our temporary perch on earth, to there, our real home. This is why I have a soft spot for homeless people—because the blessed ones are always homeless."

"However," he went on, "while the blessed ones are always homeless, the homeless are not always blessed."

"What's that supposed to mean?" Jenny challenged.

Father Lawrence grinned. "It means homelessness is not a blessed thing in and of itself. People aren't blessed just because they're homeless. A lot of homeless people are not blessed. They're lying, thieving, no-good, worthless bums."

"Whoa!" said Catherine. "That's kind of harsh, Father!"

"Have you ever gotten to know these folks, Catherine, or do you just hover around the soup kitchen because it make you feel good about yourself?"

Catherine crossed her arms and gave a pretty little pout.

"Just as I thought," he said. "So, back to the subject. Think about it. All God's people are vagabonds and pilgrims. From the very beginning, Adam and Eve are outcasts. Expelled from Paradise, they are strangers in the land, in need of divine protection. From then on, their sons and daughters are outcasts too: exiles from Eden."

JohnMark chuckled, " 'Exiles from Eden' sounds like the title of a classic movie."

"You're thinking of *East of Eden*," Michael challenged.

"When you read the Bible, you come across these amazing characters," Father Lawrence said, "and they're all outsiders. Noah is rejected by the worldly people, and yet he moves ahead with building what they all think is an absurd ark, preaching the coming chastisement. Abraham is called out of the luxurious cities of Babylon to wander in the Arabian desert in search of his never-never promised land. Can you think of more?"

"Sure," Michael said. "The Jews. They have this saying, 'My Father was a wandering Aramean.' "

"That's right," Father Lawrence continued. "They went down into Egypt and eventually settled there, but, did you know that some scholars believe the name 'Hebrew' comes from the Egyptian word *hapiru*, which means 'junk, rubbish, flotsam and jetsam, or just plain desert rats'—immigrants? Homeless trash. Those are God's Chosen People. It's incredible!" He laughed in amazement. "Some English guy once wrote, 'How odd of God to choose the Jews.' "

Father Lawrence was warming to his spiel: "Think about it. Guilty of murder, Moses flees from the court of Pharaoh to become a shepherd in the desert of Midian, and from there God speaks from the burning bush and calls him to lead His people away from the settled and comfortable life in Egypt to be nomads once again—stepping out in faith to embark on a dangerous trek to their promised land. It's summed up in the Epistle to the Hebrews."

At this point, he picked up his Bible, flipped it open, and read.

All these died in faith. They did not receive what had been promised but saw it and greeted it from afar and acknowledged themselves to be strangers and aliens on earth, for those who speak thus show that they are seeking a homeland.... They desire a better homeland, a heavenly one. Therefore, God is not ashamed to be called their God, for he has prepared a city for them. [Heb. 11:13-14, 16]

"Sometimes I go to these clergy meetings," he said, "and these guys have big rectories in the suburbs. One guy even has a beach house. I'm not kidding you. Another one has a boat. I don't blame them, but at the same time, it's not what you find in the Bible. God's people are wilderness wanderers."

He touched the Bible resting on his lap. "The story goes on. The Hebrew people—the desert rats—eventually settle in their promised land, but then, from among them, the prophets start preaching. These wild men preached and lived a radical message of judgment and mercy and, in doing so, revealed the truth that the castaways and runaways are subversive. They undermine the status quo and turn over the tables.

"Elijah stands up to the weak King Ahab and his wicked queen. Fleeing from their wrath, he shelters in a cave, where he hears the still, small voice of God. Elisha follows in his footsteps—a wandering seer in the wild places of the earth. Isaiah, Jeremiah, and the minor prophets follow in the great tradition—preaching against the corrupt kings and predicting their downfall. As subversive voices and signs of contradiction to the ways of the world, they not only live in the desert: they speak to the wasteland of their own decadent and rebellious society."

"Like Jesus turning over the tables in the Temple," Charlie interrupted. I've always liked that one.

Father Lawrence nodded. "This subversive voice from the wilderness is summed up in the life of John the Baptist. John gathers up the whole Old Testament tradition of wilderness wanderings and prophetic preaching, and as he does so, he prepares the way for Jesus Christ Himself, who, immediately after His baptism, is driven into the desert to be tempted—the desert where, St. Mark tells us, 'He was among wild beasts'" (1:13).

"*Where the Wild Things Are*," said Michael. "Did you ever read that book?"

"Yes!" said Jordan, "I loved that book—and that naughty little kid!"

Father Lawrence grinned and said, "I'm remembering his name."

Jordan laughed and clapped his hands, "Cool! The kid's name was Max. Right?"

Father Lawrence nodded to Jordan, "You get an A."

"Keep up with me here," he continued, turning back to his point, "because, throughout His life, Jesus is also a wilderness wanderer. No sooner is He born than He and His parents must run for their lives to escape Herod's fury. Nazareth, the archaeologists tell us, was a rural backwater: no more than a poor huddle of houses on a hillside. As Nathanael asks in John 1:46, 'Can anything good come from Nazareth?' Always on the move, the Lord constantly retreated to the wild mountains to pray all night. Remember, He said, "Foxes have dens and birds of the sky have nests, but the Son of Man has nowhere to rest his head" (Matt. 8:20).

I could see Father Lawrence was pretty passionate about this whole homelessness concept, and I could feel myself being drawn in and even really identifying with it. I had always felt like an outsider myself, and his words about God's people being the outsiders caught my imagination.

Michael, my philosophy classmate, put his hand up. "Sorry, Father, but, what's the point? We're not homeless people. We're middle-class college kids."

Father Lawrence replied, "I'm trying to kickstart something here. Trying to help you catch an idea.

"What's that?" Clarke asked. "You want us to be homeless people?"

"It's only when we realize that we're homeless that we can really begin the long journey home. You know the prodigal-son story. It was when the boy—who must have been about your age—was freezing in the mud and slop of the pigpen that he realized he would be better off at home. The old version of the Bible says that at that point he 'came to himself.'"

"Okay ..." Clarke was trying to take it all in.

"You said Jesus was one of those people," Shelby said, "but He was never in the pigpen. He wasn't a terrible sinner. He had a beautiful life."

"That's true," I jumped in, "but He became homeless to identify with us."

"Yes," Charlie said, "and there's that verse—I forget where—but it says 'He became sin for us' [see 2 Cor. 5:21]. Isn't that right, Father?"

"You got it," said Father Lawrence. "He identifies with our homeless condition and goes through it with us, and, when you think about it, He was on His own journey home."

"What do you mean?" Jenny frowned.

"He came here from His heavenly home with His Father, lived in the wilderness of this world for thirty-three years, and then, after His death and Resurrection, He finally got to go home."

"Oh, I see," Jenny nodded. "That's cool."

Father Lawrence said, "Here's where it all starts—first of all, realizing that we are homeless and that we need to make this long journey home. Once this realization hits, we next have to decide that this is the most important thing in our lives. Everything else is secondary."

"Then what?" I asked.

"Then, once you've decided that you want — no, you *need* — to go on this journey, you'll need to study the map. That's what this course is about. I'm going to show you the map. If you're up for it, we'll begin there next time. And next time let's meet at the rectory, where it's not so drafty. If you get there in time, I'll give you all some dinner."

3

The Map

The next Wednesday, we turned up at St. Monica's—and of course we were in time for dinner. Flo had made cannelloni, and we gathered around a big, beat-up dining-room table in the rectory.

Father Lawrence bustled in, took off his coat, and hung it on a hook by the kitchen door. He was rubbing his hands briskly as he came into the dining room.

He looked around, "Where are Jenny and JohnMark?"

"They're going to be here after dinner." Shelby said. "Jenny's car is in the shop, and JohnMark said he'd give her a lift, but I think they're going to grab a bite on the way over, so we can start without them."

Father Lawrence nodded, looked us over again, then crossed himself, and said grace. Flo lumbered in with a tray loaded with two steaming pans of cannelloni, baskets of garlic bread, and a big bowl of green salad. "You kids eat up," she said, then scooted back to the kitchen, and turned down the Pavarotti.

I opened the bottle of red wine I had brought and poured some out. Father Lawrence waved away the glass I offered him and joked, "Not for me, Austin. I'm too young to drink."

As Father Lawrence dished up the cannelloni and handed the plates around, he said, "Save room for a dish of Flo's tiramisu."

"What's that?" Clarke asked.

"You'll see." Catherine laughed. "It's this irresistible Italian dessert—coffee and cake and cream and everything nice."

As the others around the table chattered on, I mostly just listened, as I usually did. Shelby was headed to Salt Lake City to join some friends at a wedding on the weekend, and Charlie, Clarke, and Jordan were planning a trip to Florida, where another friend's family had a condo. They asked if I wanted to join them, and I noticed Father Lawrence watching as I declined. The fact is, I would have loved to join them at the condo in Orlando, but they were planning to hit Universal Studios theme park, and I didn't have that kind of money. There was no sense asking my dad. He'd sneer at that sort of thing and was already worried about the amount of debt I was accumulating from my college loans.

JohnMark and Jenny breezed in together just as we were helping Flo clear the dishes and serve the dessert.

"Tiramisu!" Jenny shrieked as she pulled up a chair. "I love tiramisu!"

JohnMark looked sheepish as he stood in the doorway. Jenny took two dishes of dessert from Flo, pulled out the chair next to her, and patted the seat, "Come sit down, JohnMark. You're going to love this stuff!"

As we were eating our dessert, Father Lawrence said, "Tonight I think we'd just as well stay here around the table for what I have to share with you. Are you all good with that?"

"Sure," Clarke said, "What's up? You look worried."

Father Lawrence shook his head, "Not worried. Just thinking there should be a change of plans."

Charlie said, "Are you backing out on us?"

"Not exactly," Father Lawrence said. "I just thought with you guys I ought to try something different. In the past, I've taught this course on spirituality over a twelve-week period, but with you guys, I'd like to work with you in a different way—more interactive."

"In what way?" Michael asked, cautious but curious.

"The course is based on what I call the Way of the Wilderness Warrior. It is a twelve-part plan for spiritual perfection—or union with God. The problem is, the whole thing is theoretical. I don't know how practical it is, so what I'd like to do is set out the plan for you, this week and next week, then let you find out the rest through your own research—your own way of discovery. That's the best way to learn something anyway."

"Okay," said Jordan. "I'm game. What's this map you're talking about?"

Father Lawrence said, "I learned it from an old friend of mine who is a monk at St. Bede's in Baltimore. Father Gregory trained as a scriptwriter in Hollywood, worked on a couple of movies, and did some TV work before he went to seminary and ended up as a monk."

"That's pretty cool," JohnMark said.

"What movies did he work on?" asked Clarke. "Did he work with anybody famous?"

"I think he rubbed shoulders with Mel Gibson and a few others, but he never really made the big time. God had something else for him to do."

"Like, be a priest," said JohnMark.

"That's right," nodded Father Lawrence.

"Well anyway, when he was training as a scriptwriter, Father Gregory came across the work of a guy called Joseph Campbell, who was a mythologist."

"A what?" Jenny asked, through a mouthful of tiramisu.

"He studied myths and stories from around the world—and he was also very much into the psychology of Carl Jung."

"Depth psychology," Michael pitched in. "Dreams and the subconscious and all that."

"Yes," said Father Lawrence. "And Campbell was also very interested in how the myths and legends of different cultures connected with psychology and the growth of the human spirit. He thought the myths and religious stories were the way people from ancient cultures passed on their beliefs—especially their beliefs about spirituality."

"I thought you were going to talk about a map," Jordan interrupted.

"Take it easy, will you?" Father Lawrence said. "I'm getting there."

"What's this have to do with movies?" asked Jenny.

"Well, Campbell suggested that beneath most myths and stories was one basic story: the hero's quest. His big book was called *The Hero with a Thousand Faces*. In many cultures from around the world, in many time periods, Campbell found the same pattern."

"The hero's quest?" JohnMark asked.

"Yes. And Campbell boiled this down to a simple template, which filmmakers like Steven Spielberg and George Lucas used to write their best movie scripts. Another guy, Christopher Vogler, used Campbell's work to help writers at the Disney studios refine their stories and characters. This accounts for the huge shift in movie making that happened in the 1970s. It's something you kids take for granted now. Most of the really great movies and TV series follow the hero's quest that Joseph Campbell picked out and explained."

"Where does Father Gregory fit in?" JohnMark asked.

"Well, he saw not only that the hero's quest was a good template for writing movie scripts but that it was also present in all the great Bible stories and the lives of the saints. In other words, the hero's quest is the plan for all the great stories. One story to rule them all—and the greatest story—the greatest quest is the spiritual quest."

"And this template is the map you were telling us about?" asked Michael.

"Correct. The map has twelve stages, and, in previous courses, I explained each step one week at a time. The problem is, it was all head and no action. This time, with the nine of you, I'd like to just outline the map briefly, then let you figure out the details."

"Why does the hero always have to be a guy?" Jenny complained.

"The hero is typically male," said Father Lawrence, "because the story is archetypal."

"What's that?" Charlie said.

"An archetype is a kind of universal symbol," said Michael. "A person or an object that represents something deeper and wider than himself or itself. Although he is classically a man, the hero is actually a symbol of humanity—and, individually, of every man and every woman."

"Yes," Father Lawrence said, "but there's more to it than that. Of course, both males and females can be heroes, but they go on the hero's quest in different ways. In fact, every individual also goes on the hero's quest differently. No two quests are the same. Each person is on his own journey."

"Okay," said Catherine, her interest sparked. "So what about the map?"

"The basic outline is simple. The hero leaves his—or her—Ordinary World."

"What's that?" Charlie interrupted.

"His hammock. His comfort zone. The place he grew up. Everything that is easy and secure and safe," Father Lawrence said. "He leaves his ordinary world and sets out into an unknown realm of adventure to seek a great prize of some sort."

"Like in *Treasure Island*," I said.

"Sure," Father Lawrence replied, "that and a million other stories. The prize might also be some great goal or accomplishment. To get there, he overcomes great obstacles, defeats the villains, learns about love, and, once he gets the prize, returns home again to use the great prize for the good of the loved ones he left behind."

"Frodo taking the ring to Mordor," said Michael.

"Luke Skywalker destroying the Death Star," said Clarke.

"You got it," nodded Father Lawrence.

"Don't forget all the princesses in fairy tales." said Shelby.

"And Wonder Woman" added Catherine.

"Of course," Father Lawrence agreed.

"The apostles leaving their nets to follow Christ," said JohnMark.

"Right," said Father Lawrence. "In fact, when you look again at the Bible stories, you'll see what Father Gregory was getting at. Likewise with the stories of the saints. Each, in his own way, left behind all that was familiar and secure—took the risk of faith, and set out to get the great prize of becoming a saint."

"I guess that's what the Church means by the phrase 'heroic virtue,'" JohnMark cut in. "You have to be a hero to be that virtuous, to really be a saint."

"Sure," said Father Lawrence. "Now that's the basic outline. What I want you to do at the next meeting is tell me what your ordinary world is, and I'll plan an adventure for you to go on—like a hero's quest. Are you up for that?"

I looked around at my eight friends. Michael was pondering the idea. JohnMark was nodding thoughtfully. Jenny was frowning. Shelby was smiling and nodding.

Catherine said, "How is this going to help us help others?"

Clarke nodded at that and added, "And, how will this help my career?

Father Lawrence said, "It will help you no matter what challenges life sets you."

Charlie spoke up, "So, is this turning into some kind of group therapy session?"

"God forbid!" Father Lawrence said. "More like a planning session of the *Mission Impossible* team."

Jordan laughed and started humming the famous theme.

"Is this the first stage of the journey?" I asked.

"What, tonight's session?" asked Father Lawrence.

"Yes."

"No. This is what, in the movie outline, is called 'the inciting incident.'"

"What's that?" Jenny asked.

"The inciting incident is the event at the beginning of the story that sets the ball rolling. It's the event—either good, bad, or indifferent—that kick-starts the action. I've decided not to teach you the whole thing but to challenge you to action. I don't know where your journeys will take you, and that's the nature of the thing. You're the ones who will find that as you go. It's the headlights of the car."

"The what?" Jenny asked.

"Headlights shine only far enough for you to see one step ahead, but they're fine if you keep moving," Father Lawrence explained.

"I get it," Charlie said. "You want us to go on this hero's quest ourselves and learn about it by experience."

"That's right," said Father Lawrence. "Who's in?"

Michael said, "I am" and then looked around at the rest of us. JohnMark nodded his affirmation.

Charlie shrugged and said, "If they can, I can." Then he poked Jordan, who shrugged and laughed, "Sure. Sounds like fun."

"Me too," Clarke added, "I'm in. Nothing ventured, nothing gained."

Shelby and Jenny looked at each other, laughed, and Shelby said, "Sure. Why not?" Catherine looked serious but nodded her agreement.

Father Lawrence looked at me, "Austin, are you in?"

"Me?" I said, looking around at my friends. "I don't know."

Father Lawrence gave me that sideways grin of his again and said, "Lord, make me a hero, but not yet?"

"Sort of."

Charlie put his arm around my shoulder, "C'mon, man!"

"Okay. Sure," I said.

What had I gotten myself into?

4

The Ordinary World

Over the next week, the nine of us couldn't stop discussing Father Lawrence's mysterious plan.

The next Wednesday we arrived, as before, to a fantastic supper, courtesy of Flo's genius. When I got there, Shelby and Jenny were setting the table, and Jordan was pulling a huge tray of baked pasta out of the oven for Flo and singing "Nessun Dorma" along with Pavarotti. Catherine was gathering the silverware, and Michael was opening a bottle of red wine. As we were about to join Father Lawrence in the dining room, JohnMark, Clarke, and Charlie breezed in.

After the meal, Father Lawrence invited us into his living room. The girls nabbed the sofa while Charlie and Clarke took over the two armchairs facing each other across a coffee table. Michael and JohnMark started to bring some chairs from the dining room while I held the door. Jordan sat on the floor, leaning against Charlie's armchair, and Father Lawrence took one of the dining-room chairs and placed it facing the girls on the sofa, with Charlie and Jordan to his left, and Clarke to his right. JohnMark and Michael placed their chairs at either end of the sofa, and I sat myself on its big round arm between Michael and Catherine.

"Okay," said Father Lawrence, interrupting our chatter. "This session is about the hero's Ordinary World. I'm going to give a little spiel about it; then it'll be your turn. You're each going to have a few minutes, and I'll tell you more about that in a minute. Everybody good with that?

"Sure," we all chimed in.

"You know how I said Father Gregory tied all this into movies?"

We nodded, and he continued, "You know how so many movies begin: the camera pans over the living room in an ordinary home, and you know you are being introduced to the main character. On the mantelpiece, the camera draws your attention to the hero's family photographs. On the shelf are his football trophies, on the wall his high school diploma, his certificates of achievement, and prom pictures. There's a dog asleep on the rug and, hanging over the back of the chair are the clothes he just changed out of. In a few short moments, we know what we need to know about the hero. He or she is an ordinary person like us: a family member, a member of society—a little bit untidy and still a work in progress.

"The hero's Ordinary World is his home and comfort zone," Father Lawrence continued. "It is a place of safety and security, where he is surrounded by familiar faces, friends, and family. It is furnished not only with sofas, chairs, beds, and dining tables but also with a ready-made set of beliefs and assumptions about reality.

"Those beliefs and assumptions are the hero's heritage. They're the grid through which he filters the world. They give structure, purpose, and meaning to his life, and, as such, they also contribute to the hero's sense of security and belonging. Can you think of any examples where the story begins like this?"

"Sure," Jordan volunteered, "one of my favorites—*Back to the Future*. The opening scene is Marty McFly's room. He's an ordinary American high school kid."

"At the beginning of the *Lord of the Rings* trilogy, we see Frodo Baggins at home in the Shire," Michael said.

"Right," said Father Lawrence. "If I remember correctly, there's a scene in which we see him with his friends, Samwise, Merry, and Pippin, swilling a pint in the pub, and the advantages and disadvantages of the ordinary world unfold in the conversation around the table. Frodo and his friends are enjoying a drink, while the old-timers talk about the danger of going on a long journey 'like that Mr. Bilbo—he was cracked.'"

Jenny said, "What about *The Sound of Music?*"

"That fits the pattern perfectly, and because it's a Catholic film, it's even better. Maria's Ordinary World is the convent."

Jenny laughed. "Yeah, but it's not really her comfort zone, is it?"

Father Lawrence agreed, "Right. How do you solve a problem like Maria? We know from the start she doesn't exactly fit in there. The hero is at home in his Ordinary World, but, like Maria, he also sticks out like a sore thumb. He's 'a problem to be solved.' The benefit of the Ordinary World is that it is safe and secure, but that is also its problem. The hero loves it, and all his friends in it, but he knows deep down there is more to life, and he knows he must set out to find it, even though, within his Ordinary World, he does not yet know what that 'something more' might be."

Michael muttered something.

"What's that, Michael?" asked Father Lawrence.

"Socrates."

"What about him?"

"He said, 'The unexamined life is not worth living.' I guess the hero knows that."

"Absolutely he knows that," said Father Lawrence, "and do you remember the famous quote by Henry David Thoreau?"

"What's that?" Michael asked.

"The mass of men lead lives of quiet desperation."

Michael nodded. "Oh yeah."

"The hero wants to know whether his fellow inhabitants of the Ordinary World ever move beyond gossip and small talk. He knows on some level that they're all living lives of quiet desperation. Do they ever ask the big questions: 'Why are we here?' 'What is the meaning of it all?' 'What is my purpose in life?' He knows there must be more to life than the humdrum monotony of his Ordinary World, and this restlessness motivates him to start looking for what is missing."

"They should all just be philosophy majors, eh, Michael?" I put in.

"Well, I feel sorry for this so-called hero," Jenny said. "He sounds like a loser."

"A loser and a loner," said Shelby—on the sofa between Catherine and Jenny.

"Thanks," said Michael, "for calling me and Austin losers and loners."

"Oh, well, I didn't mean you guys!" Shelby said.

"Shelby has a point," Father Lawrence said. "The hero is a kind of loner—but I wouldn't say he's a loser. The way the stories show him to be a loner and an extraordinary person is that the storytellers so often portray him as an orphan. Shelby's right. He *is* alone in the world. Take a moment to think about it. In fact, why don't you each come up with a hero of a movie or book who is either an orphan or comes from a broken family? You have two minutes."

Immediately, Jordan said, "I can think of dozens. Spider-Man to start with."

Jenny giggled. "Spider-Man! How old are you, twelve?"

Father Lawrence said, "Do you have an orphan hero yet, Jenny?"

She looked embarrassed, then blurted out, "I was thinking of Cinderella."

Jordan guffawed. "How old are *you*? Seven? Yeah, Cinderella you can have, but you have to admit that Spider-Man is not so dumb. Lots of the superheroes are orphans."

Charlie said, "Don't take all of them, Jordan. Superman's mine. He comes from another planet and is brought up on a farm in Kansas by his foster family."

"Just like Dorothy in *The Wizard of Oz*!" said Shelby. "She was brought up on a farm in Kansas by her aunt and uncle."

"And Luke Skywalker," added Charlie, "brought up by his aunt and uncle on the planet Tatooine."

Jenny laughed again, "What a nerd! He even knows the name of the planet!"

Charlie gave her a withering look.

"Mine's Batman," said Michael. "Remember? Bruce Wayne's parents are murdered, and he's brought up by Alfred the butler."

"I'm thinking of Joseph in the Old Testament," said JohnMark. "Not exactly an orphan but sold into slavery by his own brothers. Then there's Moses, who was sent down the river, and the boy Samuel, who is separated from his parents."

"Excellent!" said Father Lawrence. "Austin?" He looked at me.

"Huckleberry Finn?" I asked.

"That works. Catherine? Clarke?"

Catherine chewed her bottom lip and racked her brain, "Hang on. I've got one! Little Orphan Annie!"

Clarke said, "I'm not losing this one. What about those Charles Dickens characters? Pip from *Great Expectations* and Oliver Twist?"

"Dickens loved orphan heroes," Father Lawrence said. "He knew they capture the readers' attention and compassion. Now, this stuff about the orphan hero is more important than just being a trick of a good storyteller. The orphan hero has a loneliness deep within himself, and that loneliness is a sign that he is already an outsider. He is a misfit and an alien in the Ordinary World. Furthermore, sometimes his status as an outsider is marked by some weakness or disability. Maybe he is a spindly nerd, a nearsighted or physically awkward geek. Maybe he is a low achiever or has behavior or addiction problems or a disability or some physical oddity."

"Yes," Jordan said, "Peter Parker is a geek."

"And Clark Kent is a nerd," said Charlie.

"You're not a nerd, Clarke!" Catherine smiled.

"Thanks, sweetie," said Clarke, turning on his Tom Cruise smile. "You had me at 'hello.'"

Catherine blew him a kiss, and Father Lawrence continued, "All the heroes have this weakness, whatever it might be. However, if the hero has a flaw, he also has some special gift that confirms his unusual, outsider status. He is smarter or stronger. He is more insightful or spiritual. He is more courageous or competent. He is more daring, and more dangerous.

"Be that as it may, while the hero is more gifted than others in the Ordinary World, he is also more deeply flawed, and the flaw is the shadow side of his gift. He may be smarter, but he is also more arrogant. He may be more spiritual, but he is also more of a dreamer. He may be stronger but also more aggressive. He may be more courageous but also more foolhardy. He may be more determined but also more stubborn. He may be more loving but also more lustful. The paradoxical clash in his character presents the hero with one of the great challenges in the quest to come.

"This is the quest I'm going to set up for each of you. It is an outer journey, certainly, in your engagement with the world around you, but, more importantly, it is an inner journey. Father Gregory told me once that, when he was studying the craft of storytelling as part of a screenwriting course, the tutor said, 'Your hero must grow from his wound.' In other words, it is the hero's weakness and vulnerability that provide the opportunity for growth, development of character, and moral maturity. If the hero is an orphan, then it is from that wound that he will search for love. If the hero is proud and arrogant, then it is from that wound that he must learn humility. If the hero is pursued by the wolves of lust, then it is from that wound that he must learn chastity and find true love.

"It is in the Ordinary World that the hero's wound first makes itself known to the hero. He becomes aware of the yawning gap in his life and realizes that he has a need. This is why the Ordinary World—although it seems to be a world of contentment and calm, is actually, for the hero, a realm of discontent, restlessness, anxiety, guilt, and blame.

"It is from within his Ordinary World that the hero hears the 'call to adventure,' but more on that next week. For now, I want to hear about each of your ordinary worlds. Who's going to go first? Why don't we start with Charlie and go around the circle?"

"What am I supposed to say?" Charlie was embarrassed.

"Look," said Father Lawrence, "you're all going to graduate in a few short months, about to break out of the pattern that has been your Ordinary World up until now—that is, where you've come from and where you are now. That's all."

"Okay," began Charlie. "My family are Protestant Christians, as I guess you guys know. I have two brothers—one older and one younger. I usually win the fights. I like wrestling and rock climbing. That's it. Hey! I guess I already left that Ordinary World when I became a Catholic. So call me a hero."

Everyone laughed. Father Lawrence said, "Starting an adventure is easier than finishing it. What is your Ordinary World right now?"

Charlie reddened. "I guess my Ordinary World right now is that I'm not sure what I'm supposed to do with my life, so ... I drink too much instead of figuring it out." He looked away, and I was a little embarrassed to see he was tearing up.

Father Lawrence picked it up, "Okay, a little confession there. That's a good start. Jordan?"

Jordan swallowed, looked around at us, and said, "My Ordinary World is that I was brought up by my mom and grandmother after my dad walked out on us. My mom worked two jobs to keep me in Catholic school, and Grandma was always there to look after me. They're both terrific. Does that qualify me for orphan-hero status?"

"No way!" Jenny said. "At least your dad is still alive. My dad dropped dead from a heart attack when I was fifteen."

"Seriously?" Shelby said. "You never told me that!"

"It's true," said Jenny. "The guy you met who I call Dad is my stepdad. My mom remarried."

"Wow," Catherine muttered next to me. "I guess she wins the orphan-hero contest."

Father Lawrence went on again, "Okay, Jordan, and what's your Ordinary World now?"

"I'm getting a degree in dramatic production, and I want to get into film and television graphics. But, I'm not really into that world yet. That's where I want to go."

"Michael?"

"My family's pretty ordinary. My dad works in marketing for a construction company. My mom is a stay-at-home mom. She homeschooled me and my little brother and sister. Mass every week. Me and Jimmy were both altar boys. My Ordinary World now is that I'm a philosophy major, and I guess I'm that loner/loser you were talking about. I don't do much more than read my books."

Jenny was next, but she said, "I'm sorry, Father Lawrence, but I don't get where all this is going. I told you about my family, but I don't think they're dull and uninteresting, and I don't think I'm so special. Maybe I'm not cut out for this hero thing. My Ordinary World is that I'm a special-education major and I just want to get a job teaching kids with special needs. Is that so dumb?"

Father Lawrence smiled, "Not at all. That's fine, and it's okay to be skeptical. Shelby?"

Shelby brushed her hair back with her hand and said, "My mom and dad fight all the time, but I think they love each other, and they've always been good to me and my two sisters. We always went to church, but it was kind of routine. I didn't give it much thought before I came to St. Monica's, where the Mass is so beautiful. That's my Ordinary World, and the one I'm in now is that I am an art-history major and I'd love to work in art restoration somehow."

Catherine said, "I'll tell you my Ordinary World. My dad is a journalist with the *Columbia Herald*, and I'm an only child. My mom is an interior designer who works as a freelancer with big architecture firms. I'm not really any kind of hero either. I'm an English major, and I'd like to maybe teach high school English here in Charleston."

"That sounds pretty heroic to me," Father Lawrence said. "Austin?"

I shrugged, "My family is working-class. My dad's a truck driver, and he thinks it's dumb that I'm a philosophy major. I used to go to church just to please my mom, but then Charlie brought me to St. Monica's, and now this is my Ordinary World. I actually look forward to just being here, because I think this is where I am accepted for who I am, and that means a lot to me."

I looked over to see Charlie giving me his big grin and a thumbs-up, and Catherine reached up to give my shoulder a nice squeeze. Then I looked to my left at JohnMark, who said, "I was an altar boy too, and you all probably think I'm definitely going to seminary, but I'm having second thoughts about that, so that's my Ordinary World. Kind of confused and wondering what's next."

Clarke was last, and we all turned to look at him. He shrugged, and said, "I'm with Jenny on this. I'm not sure I buy all this 'leaving the Ordinary World' stuff. My Ordinary World is pretty good. My dad is an attorney, and my mom has her own business helping old people in their homes. I have three siblings—two brothers and a sister. Both brothers are headed to law school, and when I'm done here, I'm going to get my MBA and join my uncle's wholesale food firm. That's my Ordinary World, and to tell you the truth, I don't feel like an outsider in it. I don't feel like an orphan, and I don't feel like everybody else in it is inferior to me. I'm willing to come and hear what's happening next week, but I'm not sure I'm ready for what might come next." He looked embarrassed and added, "I don't mean to offend anybody—especially you, Father Lawrence. I'm sorry if I'm missing something or coming across all wrong."

Father Lawrence said, "You've all been honest, and that's what matters. Clarke, if this isn't for you, don't worry. However, I've found that the ones who resist the adventure at the beginning are the ones—in the long run—who are usually the greatest heroes."

He paused, took a deep breath, glanced at his watch, and looked around the room, bringing his hands together. "Okay, so, next week, same time?"

We nodded, and he said, "Good. Now let's go back in the kitchen. I think I can smell the coffee and cake Flo's been working on."

5

The Call to Adventure

The next Wednesday night, we all gathered together for the final session. I was enjoying the routine of a decent Italian dinner with Father Lawrence and my friends, and I wasn't sure I wanted the sessions to end, but I was curious to know what Father Lawrence had up his sleeve.

He started right in after we took our places in the living room. "All right, so, as I've told you all before, this map that I'm talking about is called 'The Way of the Wilderness Warrior.' We've already talked about the fact that God's people are nomads — wilderness wanderers — people who belong to another country, but those wanderers are warriors too. All through the Old Testament, the pilgrim people are engaged in battle."

Father Lawrence reached for his Bible and flipped it open. "Listen to this," he said, and he began to read: "'Blessed be the LORD, my rock, who trains my hands for battle, my fingers for war.' That's the beginning of Psalm 144, one of my favorites," he grinned, "and it's everywhere. All through the Psalms, the Hebrews talk about God being their shield, their fortress, and their mighty captain. It's there in the New Testament too."

He flipped toward the back of the Bible and read a longer passage:

Finally, draw your strength from the Lord and from his mighty power. Put on the armor of God so that you may be able to stand firm against the tactics of the devil. For our struggle is not with flesh and blood but with the principalities, with the powers, with the world rulers of this present darkness, with the evil spirits in the heavens. Therefore, put on the armor of God, that you may be able to resist on the evil day and, having done everything, to hold your ground. (Eph. 6:10–13)

Suddenly, he was super serious. "Look, kids, I don't know if you have realized it or not, but our country and really our whole world are drifting into darkness. It's in our culture, and it's in our Church too. You may have heard that I've been involved in some of those battles. I can tell you, it's not pretty. The enemy is all around us, and I'm not being paranoid when I tell you that you had better wake up. If you take your faith even a little bit seriously, then you had better prepare for battle, and the battle means becoming saints—mighty Wilderness Warriors.

"You know, one of the things that gets my goat about Catholicism is the prevalence of the portrayal of sissy saints. You know those holy cards, where the saint has rosy cheeks and a simpering smile? Don't you hate those?"

"Yeah," said Charlie, "or those stained-glass windows of Jesus with long blond hair, cuddling a baby lamb. Give me a break."

"Too much of that, and you'll get the impression that saints are weaklings, but they're not weaklings. They're warriors. They're toughened for battle."

Father Lawrence picked up a notepad and said, "I guess you guys have heard of C. S. Lewis. He said this: 'Enemy-occupied territory—that is what this world is. Christianity is the story of how the rightful king has landed, you might say landed in disguise, and is calling us to take part in a great campaign of sabotage.'[1]

"Instead of remembering that we are in enemy-occupied territory," he went on, "Christians have become fat and comfortable and have forgotten the battle."

"Enemy territory has become their Ordinary World," Charlie interjected.

Father Lawrence nodded grimly. "St. Paul knew what it was all about. He was engaged in the battle every day. Listen to what he went through." He went back to his Bible and said, "This is St. Paul speaking, in his Second Letter to the Corinthians." He took a moment to find the page, cleared his voice, and started to read:

> Are they ministers of Christ? (I am talking like an insane person.) I am still more, with far greater labors, far more imprisonments, far worse beatings, and numerous brushes with death. Five times at the hands of the Jews I received forty lashes minus one. Three times I was beaten with rods, once I was stoned, three times I was shipwrecked, I passed a night and a day on the deep; on frequent journeys, in dangers from rivers, dangers from robbers, dangers from my own race, dangers from Gentiles, dangers in the city, dangers in the wilderness, dangers at sea, dangers among false brothers; in toil and hardship, through many sleepless nights, through hunger and thirst, through frequent fastings, through cold and exposure. (11:23–27)

"So, if you are going to set out on this adventure of following Christ," he continued, "St. Paul here is your example. Listen to

---

[1] C.S. Lewis, *Mere Christianity* (London: Harper Collins, 1955), 47.

what else he says, this time to the Philippians." And he read for us again:

> Join with others in being imitators of me, brothers, and observe those who thus conduct themselves according to the model you have in us. For many, as I have often told you and now tell you even in tears, conduct themselves as enemies of the cross of Christ. Their end is destruction. Their God is their stomach; their glory is in their "shame." Their minds are occupied with earthly things. But our citizenship is in heaven, and from it we also await a savior, the Lord Jesus Christ. (3:17-20)

"Whoa!" Charlie said, "I never heard those passages read in the megachurch. That's pretty serious stuff."

"You bet it is," said Father Lawrence. "And it's no coincidence that in the great stories and myths, the hero is also a warrior. In one way or another, he rises up to fight against evil—and that's what lies at the heart of every great story. There's no story unless you get that conflict."

"Hang on!" Jenny said. "What about love stories?"

"There's always some obstacle for the lovers to overcome, right?"

Jenny nodded, "I guess so."

"Take one of the great love stories—*Pride and Prejudice*."

"I love that one," Catherine said.

"I do, too," said Shelby, "but Elizabeth Bennett isn't a Wilderness Warrior."

"Sure she is," said Michael. "She and her family are poor, and she doesn't fit in with all the polite society people. She's smarter than all of them and stands out from the crowd, right?"

"I guess so," said Shelby.

"And what about the way she fights with Darcy and Mr. Collins," said Jenny.

"And that awful snob—you know—the rich old lady," added Shelby.

"Lady Catherine de Bourgh," said Michael with a grin.

"Yes, that's the one!" said Shelby.

Father Lawrence said, "Yep. Virtually every famous story has a Wilderness Warrior as the hero, no matter the age or circumstances in the tale. There are four types of battle: hero against man, hero against himself, hero against nature, and hero against God, and often it's a blend of a couple of these types. It's the same with the saints. They rise above the common crowd and go on a great quest, leaving their Ordinary World to engage in a great battle to climb the mountain of perfection."

"Back to perfection again," said Clarke. "I'm doubtful."

I interrupted. "Father Lawrence, you've been talking about this map, and this adventure, and now you're telling us that it's a battle, and I get all that, but what's next? Where's this map you're talking about?"

"It's a plan or a template for the great story, and if you know it, you'll be able to set out on your own journey and have the basic outline of what to expect. We've already discussed the first steps. You'll have to discover the rest for yourself.

"The first stage, as you know, is the Ordinary World. The second stage is Hearing the Call. The call comes from within the hero's Ordinary World, and it seems to come out of nowhere. St. John Cassian—who was a monk in the fourth century—recognizes three ways the call comes to a person. Sometimes it comes directly from God, sometimes through the encouragement or inspiration of another person, and sometimes through some crisis in the person's life. But whichever means it comes from, when you push it a little, you realize that it ultimately originates from within the hero's life—through the hero's personality and desires."

"So, how do you hear the call?" Jordan asked. "And how do you know if it's really what you should do or not?"

"You have to figure that out for yourself," Father Lawrence answered. "Everybody's call is different, and everybody's journey is unique, because God made all of us as individuals. He doesn't want two identical saints. Again, it's like a map. You can have a map for your trip from South Carolina to New York City, and you can all follow the same map, but each one of you will have a different journey. You'll stop in different places, meet different people, and face different challenges."

"I get it," Michael said. "You need the map for the journey, but the map is not the journey."

"Right," Father Lawrence said. "It's like the rules for the game, or the musical notes on the page. The notes are not the music, and the rules are not the game, but you can't have the music without the notes, or the game without the rules.

"There are two levels of the call," he went on. "The first is the general call. That is the call every one of the baptized must hear because it is part of the deal of being a disciple of Christ. The general call is simple. Jesus says, 'Leave your Ordinary World and follow me,' and this will mean hardship because He also says, 'If you do not take up your cross and follow me, you cannot be my disciple'" (see Luke 14:27).

"Is that it?" Clarke asked.

"Well, there's a bit more to it. It's what the Church calls 'the universal call to holiness.' Jesus says to His disciples, 'You must be perfect, as my Father in heaven is perfect.'" (see Matt. 5:48).

"Perfection again," grumbled Charlie.

"Father," said Catherine, "surely Jesus is using hyperbole here, isn't He?"

"Hyperbole." Jenny rolled her eyes. "Remind me."

"A literary device," said Michael. "The speaker uses exaggeration to an unrealistic level to make his point. Jesus does it all the time, doesn't He, Father? Like when He said, 'If your eye offends you, gouge it out.' And then talks about how it's better to be blind your whole life than it is to sin and go to Hell. I think Catherine has a good point. Jesus' saying we have to be perfect must be hyperbole."

Father Lawrence said, "That's not what the Church teaches. John Paul II said the call to holiness is for everyone and that the lives of the saints show that it is possible. That is part of the general call. Get used to it."

"I can't be perfect," said Shelby, "and I don't think it's realistic to expect me to be."

"Of course you can't be perfect," said Father Lawrence. "The whole point is that you can't do it on your own. You have to rely on God's power—His grace, which enables you to pursue perfection. We work with His grace. Grace is like the gas in your car. The car won't go without the gas, but it also won't go on its own. You have to get in, turn it on, and drive the darn thing."

Jordan said, "That's pretty awesome, isn't it? To think that everyone who says he or she is a Christian is supposed to be shooting for perfection. But it's a far cry from reality, isn't it, Father? I mean, look around at the Church. I don't see much perfection."

Father Lawrence said, "Oh, I don't know. I see a lot of people who I suspect have reached that point, but they're humble. They don't stick out or draw attention to themselves. They're in the pews, day by day, praying, and in the soup kitchens and food pantries, in their homes and workplaces. They're far more advanced than they think they are, and they're God's secret agents—He's using them far more than all the famous Catholics."

"Why don't people recognize them then?" asked Jenny.

"I think I know," said Michael. "It's because a truly holy person is natural, and what is natural doesn't stick out.

"What do you mean?" Jenny frowned.

"Let's say the weather is clear, and the sky is blue, and you're out on a hike in the woods," Michael said. "You might say to your friend that it's a beautiful day, but you don't think it is remarkable, because it's natural. The weather and the woods are doing what is normal and beautiful and good. It's when the thunder and lightning start up that you complain and run for cover."

"Except the thunder and lightning are natural too," Clarke added.

"Okay, maybe that's not the best example," Michael conceded.

"For the natural person, the thunder and lightning aren't bad. They're part of the whole picture," I said, finally contributing to the conversation

"Yes," joined Michael, my fellow philosopher. "It's true. You need shadows as well as light. In fact, it's the light that produces the shadows."

"Deep," Jordan remarked, raising his eyebrows and nodding. "Deep."

"What Michael's getting at," said Father Lawrence, "is that goodness, truth, and beauty are what we expect, so when we meet saintly people, they don't strike us as unusual. They just seem like super-nice, happy, kind people."

"I like that," Catherine said quietly. "I think my grandmother was one of those."

"Yeah," said Jordan. "Mine too."

"That's the general call," said Father Lawrence, "to follow Christ on the path to perfection—to live in Him, and He in you. Then there is the particular call. That's how each individual is called to live out the general call."

"So, we're all called to follow Christ to the summit of perfection," said JohnMark. "We just have to figure out how we're going to do that."

"You got it," said Father Lawrence. "The individual call is how we flesh it out—how the general call becomes real, and that journey is often difficult, long, and full of trouble. My own path, for instance, had lots of false starts. I guess you know I started out in the Marines."

"You're kidding!" Jordan said.

"Really, Father?" asked Charlie. "The Marines?"

"That's right," Father Lawrence nodded. "At that point, I had no idea about the call, the idea of the Wilderness Warrior, or the demand for perfection, but I soon realized that a long career in the Marine Corps was not the life for me, so I tried the state police. After I took a bullet in my leg, I got to thinking long and hard, and that's when I started to take the spiritual journey seriously and ended up going to seminary."

"I never knew all that!" I said.

"Some people would say joining the Marines and the police were both mistakes, false starts, but God brings it all home. If we have just a little bit of our will inclined to do His will, then He uses everything—even our bad choices—as part of the plan. There's that verse in Romans, "We know that all things work for good for those who love God, who are called according to his purpose" (8:28).

"So, hear the call, try to love God, and everything will be all right," said Jenny.

"Yep." Father Lawrence nodded.

"Then, why try for perfection?" Jenny asked.

"Because perfection is your destiny," he replied simply.

"And, if you don't do the work of purification now, you'll have to do it in Purgatory, right, Father?" JohnMark said.

"Yes, but it's easier now, while you still have a physical body."

"I have a question," Catherine said. "How do we figure out the individual call?"

Father Lawrence laughed, "That's what I'm going to give you this evening. This is our last session, so I have written down nine individual calls—one for each of you."

"What!" said Clarke. "What are you talking about?"

Father Lawrence lifted a small carved, wooden box from the floor beside his chair and put it on the coffee table in front of the sofa. "In that box is a small envelope for each of you, with a name and a location. Do you want to open the box and get your envelopes?"

6

Refusing the Call

Shelby was sitting in the center of the sofa, so she reached for the box and put it on her lap—holding the lid closed. "So what's this all about, Father?" She frowned.

Father Lawrence laughed and said, "I've got a challenge designed for each one of you. I'm going to be bold and give you a call to adventure. It's not *the* call. You'll have to get that from God later on, but it's a shove in the right direction. This is the way I've chosen to introduce you to the next steps in the Way of the Wilderness Warrior. So, are you game or not?"

"Sure!" Jordan said, jumping up and grabbing the box from Shelby.

"Hey! Give that back!" she yelled.

When she got up and grabbed for the box, Jordan tossed it across the room to Clarke, and when Catherine jumped up to grab it from Clarke, he tossed it across to Charlie. Charlie tossed it to Michael when Jenny went for it, and he finally tossed it to me. I tucked it under my left arm, sat down, and opened it. Inside were nine small white envelopes with our names on them. I handed them out one by one, and we sat and opened them, like little kids on Valentine's Day.

Father Lawrence sat watching us and grinning. Jenny was the first to read hers out. "Sister Anna Grace. Dominican Convent, Nashville, Tennessee. Who's that?"

Shelby said, "Sister Gemma Cherian. Missionaries of Charity Convent, Brooklyn, New York. Who did you get, Catherine?"

Catherine read out the name on her paper: "Dame Etheldreda Laws, O.S.B., Monastery of St. Cecilia, Isle of Wight, England."

I listened as the other guys started comparing notes. Charlie said, "Father Roger Carson, Military Chaplaincy, Parris Island, South Carolina."

JohnMark's contact was Msgr. Kevin O'Donnell, St. Joseph Seminary, Dublin, Ireland.

Jordan read his out next: "Brother Vincent Fiorini, Franciscan Friars of the Renewal, The Bronx, New York City, New York."

Clarke read out, "Randolph Harrison Gordon IV, Gordon, Inez and Morganstern, 125 Fifth Avenue, Manhattan, New York."

"Michael?" Father Lawrence asked, and Michael read, "Professor James Allen Wright, Boston College, Boston, Massachusetts."

Finally, Father Lawrence turned to me and waited expectantly. I looked down at my slip of paper and read out loud, "Dom Aelred Looney, Cripple Creek Abbey, Herbertsville, Oklahoma."

And then everyone started talking all at once.

Jenny was practically screaming, "I mean, who is this person? So I'm just supposed to turn up on her doorstep in Nashville and say, 'Hi Sister. Y'know I'm looking for this map Father Lawrence told us about.'"

He laughed, "Yeah, more or less. You got the idea. Don't worry. I've got permission from them all. They know you might be in touch. Then again—you might not be in touch. It's your decision.

Clarke frowned, "Can't you tell us more about them?"

"Nope. You're smart. You'll figure it out. God will provide. All I can tell you is that each of those people knows what they are talking about, and I chose each one specifically for each of you."

"Hang on!" Shelby said. "You expect me to somehow travel to New York City, find a place to stay, then turn up at this convent? Missionaries of Charity. They're the Mother Teresa nuns, right?"

Jordan said, "Hey, I'm going to New York. We can hang out."

Clarke joined in, "I've got a New York address too. I don't know who this guy is, but he sounds like a lawyer or something."

"Stockbroker," Father Lawrence said.

Clarke said to Jordan and Shelby, "We can travel together!"

"Uh-uh." Father Lawrence shook his head. "One of the rules is that you have to travel alone. No contact until six months from now, when I'll take you all on a retreat for three days to a retreat house I know of down at Hilton Head. It'll be my treat."

"Bummer," said Jordan. "I think I'm going to change my mind."

Catherine said, "You've given me somebody in England. How am I going to pay for a trip to England, and where the heck is the Isle of Wight?"

"You'll figure it out." And he smiled.

JohnMark said, "I'm going to Ireland. We can travel together."

"Nope," said Father Lawrence. "On your own."

"Where are you going again, Austin?" asked Charlie.

"Some monastery in Oklahoma, of all places," I said. "But I don't see how I can do this. I can't just drop out of school for a semester."

"Why not?" said Father Lawrence. "Sometimes dropping out is the best option."

"What will my parents say?" I protested.

"I'm with Austin," Michael said. "We're halfway through our senior year. We can't just walk away."

"Sure you can," Father Lawrence said.

Charlie said, "In fact, the administration encourages us to take a semester away. If you ask permission, you can do that—for study abroad or external studies."

"There you go," Father Lawrence said, "external studies. Michael at Boston College, and Austin at Cripple Creek.

"I don't know about Parris Island," said Charlie. "Isn't that the Marines?"

"You bet," smiled Father Lawrence. "Semper Fi! C'mon, Charlie. Man up!"

All nine of us kept talking to each other while Father Lawrence went out to the kitchen. He came back with a tray of dishes loaded with some of Flo's famous gelato cake.

He handed the dishes around, then sat down and grinned at us, as if he had pulled off some marvelous magic trick. We started shooting questions at him: Where would we get the money? Where would we stay? How would we get there? What would people think? What would our parents say? What if we messed up? Why was he making us do this?

"I'm not making anybody do anything," he said. "Get that straight. Each one of you will choose to do this or not. It's your choice, and what is interesting is that all nine of you have already plunged into the third stage of the hero's quest. The first stage is the Ordinary World. The second stage is Hearing the Call, and what's the third stage?"

"Following the call?" JohnMark guessed.

"... is the wrong answer," Father Lawrence shook his head.

"*Answering* the call?" Catherine asked.

He made a sound like a buzzer. "Wrong!"

"Being a disciple!" Jordan ventured.

"Wrong again," said Father Lawrence. "The third stage is Refusing the Call."

"What!" protested Jenny. "How is that heroic?"

"It's actually an important part of the journey. The hero refuses the call, and if he doesn't at one point, he will at another. This is important because it means he is taking the call seriously. Each one of you came up with some reason why you can't respond to the call and follow through. That's okay. That's a good sign. It means you are not being lighthearted about this. If you're thinking through the problems, you're also already thinking through the solutions. So, questioning the call is a good thing—even though it feels bad."

JohnMark pondered for a moment, then said, "Father Henry, the director of vocations, said something similar. We were on a vocations retreat, and he said they are suspicious of men who are too gung ho about being priests. Maybe they've got romantic ideas about the priesthood, or maybe they are too full of themselves, or maybe they are using the priesthood as an escape route from reality, but the vocations advisers consider it a mark of a true vocation if the man has doubts."

Michael said, "I get it. My uncle said it's the same with marriage. If you don't think twice, you're not taking it seriously enough."

Catherine said, "That's such a guy thing to say!"

"But they're right," Shelby said. "You have to weigh things up if you wanna make the right decision. So, Father," she turned to him, "you've given me this Mother Teresa nun. What is she supposed to do for me? Are you telling me I'm supposed to be a sister in the Missionaries of Charity?"

"I'm not telling you anything. I'm just giving you a challenge. Remember what Michael said in our first session?"

"No. What did Michael say?" Shelby asked.

"You mean the Socrates quote?" Michael asked Father Lawrence, who nodded and waited for Michael to say it again.

"The unexamined life is not worth living."

"This is simply a real-life chance for you to examine life," said Father Lawrence, "to hear the call and maybe figure out your individual call. Sister Gemma is a person to help you do that."

Suddenly everyone was silent. Father Lawrence spoke up again, "I realize this seems like a game, but it's not. It is a real-life challenge. As I said, you're right to refuse the call. That's the third stage of the journey, and it is a vital stage. Next time you watch a movie, check it out. The hero will be presented with the challenge, then he'll try to back out, or find umpteen reasons why he can't do it. Then comes the fourth stage: Meeting the Mentor. The mentor is a symbolic character in all the great stories. He is often portrayed as a wise old man."

"Like Obi-Wan Kenobi," Charlie said.

"Obi-Wan is a perfect example," Father Lawrence said. "Can you all think of others from stories or movies?"

"Dumbledore," muttered Jenny.

"Merlin," said Michael.

"Gandalf is an obvious one," added Michael.

"Some of the Desert Fathers," said JohnMark.

"Who the heck are the Desert Fathers?" asked Jordan.

"The first monks in the Egyptian desert, in the fourth century," JohnMark replied.

"That old guy from *The Karate Kid*. I loved that film when I was in grade school," said Clarke.

"They are all good examples."

"Why are they always old men?" Catherine asked.

"The mentor is not always an old man—especially in real life. The mentor could be almost anyone. But in the myths and movies, the old man also functions as a symbol of wisdom. He's old because wisdom comes with age and experience. He is also old because he holds in himself the wisdom of the tribe—the inherited wisdom from those who have gone before. He's the keeper of the flame, the custodian of the tradition. An old man symbolizes that best."

"But why not an old woman?" protested Catherine.

"Because the stories function at the subconscious level," Michael said. "The old man symbolizes the patriarch – the father or the grandfather. The old woman has a different function in the story. She is the mother, the wise grandmother, the fairy godmother."

"Okay," Jenny said, "like in 'Cinderella.'"

"That's an excellent example of the feminine mentor," Father Lawrence said. "In the great stories from the Bible, mentor figures also show up. The boy Samuel has the old prophet Eli as his mentor. Elijah mentors Elisha the prophet. Ruth is mentored by Naomi, and the Blessed Virgin by St. Elizabeth."

"And the old woman Anna, in the Temple?" suggested JohnMark.

"That's another one," said Father Lawrence. He went on: "The mentor is not only a person. It is any tool, source of knowledge, skill, information, or ability the hero needs to go on the journey with confidence. The mentor trains the hero, teaches the hero, and most importantly, he loves the hero."

"What?" Clarke frowned. "That's kind of creepy, isn't it?"

"What I mean is that the mentor feels a fatherly affection for the hero. Not all love is *eros*, the romantic love that you're thinking of. The mentor believes the hero can accomplish the quest. He boosts the hero's self-esteem and confidence. He accepts the hero, sees both his faults and his strengths and wills him to succeed. That's what I mean when I say he loves the hero."

"Okay," shrugged Clarke, "I get that."

"The mentor doesn't spoon-feed the hero. He's not a babysitter or a nursemaid. He challenges the hero, helps him recognize his faults, and helps him learn self-discipline."

"Is there only one mentor?" Jordan asked.

"There could be many before the story is over," said Father Lawrence. "Luke Skywalker has Obi-Wan, but he also has Yoda. Also, the mentor has a shadow character in the story. That character is the hero's nemesis."

Jordan started humming the Darth Vader theme, then said in his deepest voice, "Luke, I am your father."

"You got it," Father Lawrence laughed. "The nemesis is the dark side of the mentor figure. He is the source of temptation, and he's the symbol of the dark side within the hero himself. That's why Luke Skywalker in *The Empire Strikes Back* goes into that cave on Yoda's planet and cuts off Darth Vader's head, but remember, when it rolls over, Luke's own face appears. So you see, the nemesis is the dark side of our *own* personalities."

"This is getting pretty deep," Charlie said.

"Are you saying these people you want us to meet are actually evil?" said Jenny.

"No. They're good, but when you meet them, you will also, in one way or another, meet someone else who will be like a mentor figure but will tempt you to the dark side of yourself. This happened to me. Do you want to hear about it?"

"Sure," Jordan said.

Father Lawrence looked around the room, saw all their waiting faces, and went on. "When I was in the police academy, training to be a state cop, I had this mentor figure who was responsible for training all of us cadets. He was an older guy who took his responsibilities seriously, and all of us loved him. He was an honorable cop and taught us the real principles of law enforcement—to serve our country and serve the people. But there was another teacher in the academy, and he tried to seduce me."

"What, was he gay?" Charlie asked.

"Not that kind of seduction," Father Lawrence said. "He was a crooked cop. He introduced me to some other guys who had a scam going on. They took bribes from organized crime families, and they tried to initiate me into their gang. It was very tempting. They were the cool guys, the ones who were going somewhere—the ones with money, women, and power. Luckily, I'd had enough secondhand experience with guys like that in the Marine Corps to recognize them for what they were and to avoid the trap."

"Do you think we'll fall for the dark side?" JohnMark asked.

"I think you'll be tempted by the anti-mentor for sure."

"Why not call him the 'tormentor'?" Jordan quipped.

Father Lawrence laughed, "Yes, good one! The tormentor will do his best to trip you up, and if you fall, you would not be the first one to stumble on the path to perfection."

"In fairy tales, I guess the wicked witch is like the dark side of the fairy godmother," said Jenny, thinking out loud.

Michael said, "But the tormentor might appear good, right?"

"Absolutely," said Father Lawrence. "The guys in the police I told you about did not come across as evil. They seemed smart and funny, on top of everything, and got along well with everyone."

"So the mentor will know our strengths," Shelby asked, "but, the tormentor will know our weaknesses?"

"It's not quite that simple. It's more like, both of them know your strengths *and* weaknesses, and because they know you, they know that your weaknesses are really only the shadow side of your strengths. The mentor tries to bring out the strengths. The tormentor tries to play on the weakness. But don't worry too much about this right now. You'll have a chance to encounter all of these challenges in good time, if you are willing to go on the journey. All you need to know now is that the names I've given you are the people I've selected to be your mentors. All of them know the

Way of the Wilderness Warrior, because all of them have been on the journey themselves. Now, just as I said in our last session, you have to decide whether you're going to take up the challenge. Don't tell me tonight one way or the other. Just decide, then go for it—or don't. If you decide to go for it, then send me a text from time to time to let me know how it's going. For now," and he paused a moment, "let's wind things up. I've given you plenty to think about."

That was an understatement. This final session of his was mind-blowing. Did I really have the guts to drop out of college for a semester to go look up this monk in Oklahoma? Was I up to it? I didn't consider myself to be any kind of hero, and I had never traveled outside South Carolina except for a family vacation once to a cabin in North Carolina. How would I tell my folks, and where would I get the money to travel to Oklahoma? And if I ever figured out how to get there, where would I stay?

As I tried to sleep that night, I could hear Father Lawrence laughing and saying, "Don't worry. You're smart. You'll figure it out. And God will provide."

7

Meeting the Mentor

The next morning, I sent Father Lawrence a text: "Can we meet? I want to ask a few questions about this quest."

He texted back immediately and offered to take me to lunch. He likes Southern food, so we met up at Clara's Kitchen—a local place with huge helpings of whatever Clara is cooking that day. It was Thursday, so it was fried catfish sandwiches, slaw, and hush puppies. Father Lawrence got ready with a big glass of sweet tea.

While we were waiting for the food to arrive, he looked at me and said, "So, what's up?"

"I know you are just trying to get us to think things through, Father Lawrence," I began, "but do you really expect the nine of us to drop everything and head off on some kind of spiritual treasure hunt?"

He shrugged, "You don't need to, but you can."

"But you've set us up for this."

"I invited you to participate. Nobody made you come to the sessions, and nobody is making you go on the quest. I'm not putting pressure on any of you. 'Do, or don't do. There is no try.' "

I laughed, "Yoda the mentor."

Clara's helper—a slim African American girl with "Shavawn" stitched on her name tag, sauntered up. "Y'all want more sweet tea?"

"Sure," said Father Lawrence holding up his cup. "Thank you."

"Your lunch is coming right up," she smiled.

"Okay," I said. "Look at that waitress there. She's probably a good Baptist who loves Jesus. Why isn't she on a quest to a monastery in Oklahoma or England?"

"If she is a follower of the Lord, then she is on her own quest. I don't know what that is, but I do know that every one of the baptized have got their own quest laid out. Perfection is our shared destiny, and while the map has some universal stages, everybody's journey is different. And remember, even though I talk about a first stage, second stage, and so forth, the stages don't necessarily come in sequential order. Any one person may experience the stages multiple times in his or her journey or may experience multiple stages simultaneously."

"What do you mean?" I asked, as Shavawn put our catfish and hush-puppy baskets on the table.

"I followed the call and refused the call several times in different ways, and I've had a number of mentors along the way. I told you about my friend Dom Gregory at St. Bede's Abbey in Baltimore. Another mentor was a retired archbishop named Ambrose. The main thing is to learn the stages of the journey and then step out and be prepared for anything to happen—and, if it's an adventure, be prepared for some discomfort and challenges. You know what Bilbo Baggins said in *The Hobbit*?"

"No. What?"

"An adventure is something that, when you are in the middle of it, you wish you were at home by the fire."

I laughed, then asked, "But why did you pick the nine of us?"

"I sensed that you were ready for the challenge—some of you more than others probably."

"Which ones do you think will accept the challenge?" I asked.

"I reckon Jordan won't take you up."

"Oh no." Father Lawrence shook his head as he considered a hush puppy. "Jordan will do just fine. So will the girls." He popped the hush puppy into his mouth.

"Even Jenny? She always seems so negative."

"She's not really negative. She's just checking things out. I might be wrong, but I think Jenny will be one who sticks it out. Michael and Charlie—maybe not so much."

"But they both seemed pretty engaged."

"Michael will start well, but I'm guessing he will probably talk himself out of it. Charlie likes the idea of a battle. If he can see it as a kind of spiritual boot camp, he'll probably see it through."

"What about JohnMark and Clarke?"

"JohnMark will struggle with what he should do and what he *thinks* he should do, and that might make him stumble. Clarke is an open question. He could be great if he adjusts his expectations, but I can see him getting distracted pretty easily."

"And what about me?"

"I thought that was what this was all about," said Father Lawrence. "You're worried. Do you want a piece of pie? Clara makes the best key lime pie in Charleston."

"Sure," I said.

"Shavawn?" Father Lawrence called.

"Yessir?"

"Can we have two slices of Clara's key lime pie over here when you get a chance?"

Shavawn was giving Julia Roberts a run for her money in the radiant-smile competition. "Sure thing!"

"Now, Austin," Father Lawrence said, looking straight into me. "What about you?"

"Yeah." I glanced away, "Do you really think I should do this?"

"What do you want to do?"

"I want to do this, but … I don't want to do this."

"That's good," said Father Lawrence. "What does your heart say?"

"Do this."

"What does your head say?"

"This is dumb. Don't be crazy."

"Which do you trust more—head or heart?"

Shavawn brought the pie, and I started in, stalling. But, after a bite, I burst out, "I don't know. I really don't know."

He chuckled, "I think you do. You trust your heart. If you didn't, you would not have signed up for my course to start with. You don't need me to hold your hand on this, Austin. You just need to find your courage and follow this lead. This is how the Holy Spirit leads us, you know."

"How?"

"There is that verse somewhere in the Bible … Charlie would know."

"Yes, he would!" I smiled.

"The verse is 'Find your delight in the Lord who will give you your heart's desire'" (Ps. 37:4).

"Charlie actually has a poster in his room with that on it," I laughed.

"Don't tell me," Father Lawrence laughed. "The text is printed over a picture of a sunset at the beach."

"Close. It's guy standing on a mountaintop with his arms outspread toward the sunrise. But what about God and desire?"

"Well," Father Lawrence continued, "I heard someone say once that God will grant you the desires of your heart, but first, He will put those desires in you."

"What?"

"God puts the desires there first; then He leads you in the path to the fulfillment of those desires."

"I get it. That's why you asked what my heart was saying."

"That's right. If you learn to look within, you'll usually know what you should do because, deep down, it's also what you want to do."

"Okay, so, what do I do next?"

He finished his pie, then said, "I'm not going to tell you — except that you need to go and meet with Father Aelred at Cripple Creek Abbey."

"Okay," and I took a deep breath, then let it out. "I'm going to do it."

"Good! Have you ever visited a Benedictine monastery before?"

"No. What's the drill?"

"You need to write to the guestmaster. That's the monk who looks after hospitality. He'll reserve a room for you."

"Do I have to pay to stay there?"

"Usually they expect people to make a donation of whatever they can, but if you're young and fit like you are, you can ask to be given work to do while you're there. That's the best thing. Work is a big part of their life anyway."

"How am I going to get there?"

"Look Austin, I'm not going to nursemaid you on this. How to get there? Take a plane to Tulsa for a start."

"How am I going to pay for it?"

"You'll figure it out," Father Lawrence said as he got up. "But I suggest you ask God about it. You know, 'Ask and you shall receive.'"

"What — just ask God for the airfare?"

"Sure, and don't forget the taxi. Cripple Creek is out in the boondocks. You'll need an extra seventy-five bucks for a taxi or an Uber or whatever. C'mon, I gotta get back."

He gave me a lift to St. Monica's, and I went into the church and did something I'd never done before: I asked God for money.

I needed about four hundred bucks for a round-trip ticket and taxi fare. While I was at it, I added an extra fifty for spending money.

The next week, one of Charlie's friends asked if he could buy the motor scooter I had used to get around Charleston. It was worth about four hundred bucks, but he offered me—you guessed it—$450.

I booked my flight to Tulsa and checked Google Maps. The monastery really was out in the sticks. It was going to be almost a two-hour drive from the airport.

I was worried what my folks would make of my crazy plan, so I took the easy way and told my mom what was up and told my academic adviser I was taking a semester to do external studies, and I booked my flight. I left my mom to inform my dad. He thought my majoring in philosophy was bad enough; the fact that I was taking a few months off to travel and stay at a monastery would really set him off. Maybe I should have just told him what I was going to do, but I figured it would be better to discuss things after all was said and done.

On a bright, cold Friday, in the first week of February, I set off on my adventure. I knew Michael was heading to Boston, and Charlie told me he had set up an appointment with his guy at Parris Island, but I hadn't spoken to the rest of my friends about the challenge. After all, Father Lawrence had said we had to travel alone, and, to be honest, I was kind of worried that I'd crash out, and I didn't want them to know.

I had to change planes in Charlotte, but otherwise the flight to Oklahoma was easy enough. After about two hours in the taxi, going down narrower and narrower roads, we turned onto a dirt track and passed through a wrought-iron gate with "Cripple Creek Abbey" in the arch over the gateway. We followed a long dirt road through a valley, across the rolling farmland of eastern Oklahoma, through a small patch of woods by a wide creek and finally crossed an arched bridge, drove up a hill, and pulled into a gravel parking lot in front of the monastery.

I climbed out and stretched and gazed at the huge abbey church to my left. It was constructed of yellow brick, and it looked only half built, still in progress. Straight in front of me was a smaller brick building with a sign that read "Bookshop and Guests."

I got my suitcase out of the trunk, paid the driver, and made my way to the bookshop. Inside were the usual racks of rosaries and holy cards, a wide selection of books about the liturgy and monasticism, and an area where they sold stuff the monks made—pottery, cheese, honey, icons, and calligraphy. A pudgy monk in black robes who looked as if he was in his mid-forties, with thinning hair and wire-rimmed glasses, was sitting on a stool behind the counter with his nose stuck in a book.

He looked up. "Can I help you?"

"Yes. I'm here for a visit. I guess, I'm supposed to ask for the guestmaster."

"You must be Austin." He smiled, "I'm Brother Boniface. I'm the guestmaster. Let's go into the church first and thank God for your safe journey. Then I'll show you to your room."

Brother Boniface took my suitcase and led me through a side door and down a corridor to the church. Even though it was only half built, it was still huge and austerely beautiful. We stood before a statue of the Virgin on the right side of the church, lit a candle, and said a Hail Mary and an Our Father together before he gestured for me to follow him through a door at the back. He led me up a flight of stairs to a hallway full of rooms; this was the guesthouse, he explained.

He opened a door into a simply furnished room. There was a throw rug on the vinyl floor, a single bed, a desk and chair, an armchair, and an open window. Outside, a bell was ringing. Brother Boniface pointed to the desk: "The schedule is there, so you'll know what to do. That's the bell for Vespers. Wait for me at the back of the church, and I'll tell you the rest."

"Should I go to Vespers?"

"You can if you want, but you might be tired after your trip. Maybe you want to rest. If so, come back down to the church in about a half hour and I'll meet you then."

After Boniface had gone, I stretched out on the bed, but I couldn't sleep. So I found my way back to the church. I slipped as quietly as possible into the back and listened to the monks singing the psalms in Gregorian chant. This was more restful than a nap. I was soon caught up in the ethereal rhythms and harmonies, and I guess I drifted into prayer—although maybe I was just having that nap I needed.

After Vespers, Brother Boniface showed me the monastic dining room—the refectory—and explained about the mealtimes and the daily routine. The monks got up at five o'clock for Matins—the first office of the day. Then, after a little breakfast, they gathered together for Lauds, their morning prayer. There was time for work, then Mass was at ten o'clock, followed by meditation and reading. After lunch, the monks went out to work more. There was a short, midafternoon office, then Vespers at five o'clock. After supper, the monks met for a time of recreation, then ended the day with Compline, their nine o'clock night office.

After Boniface explained the routine, I decided there was no time like the present to be bold, so I went right ahead and told him, "I have come here on a special quest—if that doesn't sound too weird."

"What's that?" He smiled.

"I'm supposed to meet up with Dom Aelred Looney."

Brother Boniface burst out laughing, "What! Looney Tunes?"
I frowned. I didn't expect monks to have nicknames for each other.

"Oh, don't worry!" He laughed when he saw my face. "Everybody calls Father Aelred 'Looney Tunes'—even Father Abbot."

"Why is that?" I asked.

"Because dear old Father Aelred is a bit—what do you say? Looney? Maybe it's dementia, or maybe he's just a bit eccentric. Are you sure it's him you've come to see, and not Father Jacob?"

"Who is Father Jacob?"

"He's the one everybody wants for a spiritual director. He's written a couple of books, and they made a TV show about him. Father Jacob is famous, but he's not a monk here anymore. He visits, but he has his own ministry away from Cripple Creek. Sure it wasn't him you're supposed to meet?"

"No," I said, "it was definitely Father Aelred Looney."

Brother Boniface frowned, "Okay, but I'm not sure you'll be able to meet him."

"Why not?"

"Because he's a hermit. He doesn't live here. He lives a few miles down the lane in his own place."

"I really think I should try to meet him. It's important that I at least try."

"Okay," said Brother Boniface, "I'll see if I can get permission from Father Abbot. Father Aelred asks for all visitors to be approved by Father Abbot first."

The next day, after lunch, Brother Boniface found me a pair of overalls and work boots, and I joined three other monks— Brothers. Matthew, James, and Nicholas—repairing one of the long barbed-wire fences that contained the abbey's dairy cattle. All three monks were in their twenties, tanned and fit. Matthew had a broad, handsome face with a scrawny blond beard. James was tall, heavyset, and dark with a full beard. Nicholas was more of a nerd—clean shaven; pointy features; quick, darting eyes; maybe a bit shy and nervous.

All three monks were lay brothers. They explained that they weren't training to be priests, and therefore were not doing advanced theological or philosophical studies. They were full Benedictine monks, but they were the worker bees. "The lay brothers do most of the physical labor—the choir monks are the ones who become priests."

"Isn't that a bit unfair?" I asked.

They laughed, "No, we don't want to sit around reading all day, and they don't want to be out chopping wood, building a barn, or cleaning out the pigsty. They do their part, we do ours, and, ultimately, we all work together as a team."

"Why are you here?" Nicholas asked. "Are you trying your vocation as a monk?"

"Me?" I said. "No. I'm here to meet Father Aelred Looney."

Brother Matthew laughed, and I saw him slip a secret smile to the other two.

Brother Nicholas said, "Father Looney? He lives out in the woods, on his own. He's our only hermit."

Brother James added, in a broad voice, "Everybody calls him Looney Tunes, but I think it's a bit unkind. He's just old and eccentric, that's all. My grandpa got like that when he was older."

After Vespers that afternoon, Brother Boniface met me at the back of the church and said, "Father Abbot has given permission for you to visit Father Aelred. I'll take you over there after Lauds tomorrow morning."

The next morning, after Lauds, I climbed into one of the beat-up old pickup trucks the monks used to get around the property, and Brother Boniface chatted as we bounced down the dirt road, dodging potholes until we reached the main road.

He told me about Dom Aelred as he drove. "Father Aelred is one of the founding members of the community. As a young college student at the University of Kansas, he went to France with some friends, and they ended up becoming Catholics and joining an old monastery there, Fontgombault. It was a pretty big adventure, as they were all young Americans who didn't even speak French. But Father Aelred persevered, and about twenty years ago, he came back to the States with five other monks and established Cripple Creek."

We turned right off the main road, and as we dodged the potholes and ruts to head down a steep incline into a little wooded valley, I understood why the shocks on the truck were shot. Brother Boniface jolted to a stop, pulled on the hand brake, and climbed out. "We go on foot from here," he said.

A little footpath took us down through a copse of trees to a brook at the bottom of the valley. The brook was dammed up to create a small, shallow pond. Nestled there, on the other side of the pond, was a tiny log cabin with a fieldstone chimney on the left side. A skein of smoke drifted up from the chimney, and as we stood at the side of the pond, Brother Boniface whispered, "Father Aelred built the hermitage himself. He felled the trees, gathered the stones for the chimney and," he laughed, "begged, borrowed, and stole the rest of the building materials from the abbey church building site."

As we walked around the pond and used stepping-stones to cross the brook, I saw a garden to the right of the cabin, surrounded by a fence woven from saplings. An old man in a monk's habit stood next to a pile of freshly split logs, and I saw him raising an axe over his head, preparing to chop through a log standing upright on the chopping block.

Brother Boniface waited till he finished the swing, then called out, "Peace be with you."

"And with your spirit," the old man mumbled automatically as he lowered the axe. He looked up, and gave Boniface a quick, sprightly smile of welcome. A grey woolen hat was perched on his bald head. His rosy face was framed with a circlet of white, collar-length hair, and a wispy chin beard. We opened the gate, and as I got closer, I saw he was sporting an embroidered Porky Pig badge and a Looney Tunes logo on the front of his hat.

The old monk caught my eye and said, "You must be Austin Fairfax."

I nodded, and he smiled and said, "What a fine name!" He gestured to the door, busied himself with removing his hat and apron, and said, "You'd better come in. I've been expecting you."

8

The Turning

Father Aelred took my arm and led me to the cottage. He nodded
to Boniface, who simply smiled at me and said, "I need to get back.
I guess Father Aelred will give you some lunch. I'll pick you up
later this afternoon."

There was a log fire blazing on the hermitage hearth, and the
little one-room cottage was filled with smoke. He opened the door
and, waving his hands, struggled to open the windows.

"I'm sorry," he said, in a high-pitched voice with the trace of
what I thought was a French accent. "The fireplace doesn't draw
properly. Sometimes it gets a bit smoky when there's a downdraft."

I looked around as the smoke cleared. The back and right walls
of the room were lined with bookshelves from floor to ceiling. On
the right wall, facing the fireplace, there was a space between the
bookshelves for a little altar with an antique silver crucifix on the
wall above. On the altar were candlesticks, and on a small bookshelf
next to a prayer desk were all the books and gear for prayers and
Mass. Hanging to the left of the prayer desk were vestments. The
back right corner of the room was partitioned off with bookshelves.
Behind a curtain I could see a simple bed and a bedside table with
a lamp and another pile of books. The corner of the cabin to the
left, at the back, held a simple counter with a sink, a tiny fridge,

and a gas stove fed by a propane tank. I noticed a back door that I figured must lead to an outhouse.

The main space of the room was taken up with a large table with one straight chair. The table was cluttered with more books, notebooks, a microscope, an old computer monitor, a keyboard, and a large old desktop computer tower. Wires snaked here and there connecting power, a Wi-Fi router, and who knows what else. Dust was everywhere. In front of the fire were two worn armchairs covered with colorful crocheted blankets with a small round table between them. I noticed that one leg of the table was held together with duct tape. A large, mean-looking grey cat was asleep on one of the armchairs.

Father Aelred hurried to the kitchen with a funny limping, stooped gait. He opened a cupboard and took out two large brown bottles, opened them, and bustled back with two smeared tumblers under his arms. He placed them on the table in front of the fire. He gestured for me to take the empty armchair and pushed the cat off the other one onto the floor.

"Go on, Jeoffrey," he said, sitting down. "This is my chair."

Jeoffrey yowled in protest and tried to scratch him.

"Ungrateful beast," Father Aelred muttered, pulling his hand away just in time. "Do you know Smart?" he asked, looking straight at me.

"Smart? Do you mean, am I smart?"

He laughed. "Of course you're smart. Father Lawrence wouldn't have sent a dunderhead to visit me. I meant, have you ever heard of Christopher Smart?"

"No. I'm afraid not, sir."

He waved his hand to me, "No need to call me sir. I'm not your master, and you're neither my son nor my slave. You can call me Brother if you like — or Looney Tunes." With that, he gave me a sly, sideways look and smiled. "I know that's what they call me. It's a good one. That's me! I am Looney by name, looney by nature!"

With that he gave a long, high-pitched giggle like a cross between the laughs of a seventh-grade girl and a hyena. I was worried. What kind of a "loon" had I traveled all this way to meet?

"Christopher Smart," he said, plopping himself down. "Eighteenth century. English poet. High churchman. They though he was crazy and sent him to the famous insane asylum Bedlam. He wrote a wonderfully weird poem about his cat Jeoffrey." At this point he gestured to his own cat, who was perched like an aristocrat on a cushion by the fire, scowling at us. "Thus the name of my familiar over there."

Then he gestured to the table with his long, thin hand. "This beer is very delicious. Did you expect me to serve you tea? Tea is for the queens of England. Too precious. Perhaps you heard of my years in France and wished for a drop of brandy? Calvados from the land of dear St. Thérèse perhaps? I have some of that if you would prefer, but I like this beer. It is brewed by our brothers in Norcia. Do you know Norcia?"

"I'm afraid not," I stuttered. "What is Norcia?"

"Not what. Where. Norcia is a place. The birthplace of our Holy Father, St. Benedict. Some of our fellow Benedictine monks have returned to Norcia, and they brew this beer. I know the brewmaster. He is a young monk from South Carolina, Father Augustine. Do you know him?"

"I don't."

"You'd like him. He has your name. Austin is a form of Augustine, you know. Is that how you got your name?"

I grinned to hide my embarrassment and gave him the same explanation I'd shared with Father Lawrence some months ago.

"How creative!" he said. "But also providential, perhaps. God moves in a mysterious way His wonders to perform. Sometimes a simple name proves to be serendipitous—or symbolic even. Do you know what my nickname was as a child?"

"No, what?"

"Monkey. My older brother, when he first saw me as an infant said, 'He looks like a monkey.' And he was right. I was a scrawny baby, and the pictures of me are simian in appearance. Anyway, the name stuck, and everyone called me Monkey, and now here I am—a monk!" Then he started in again on that high-pitched giggle, this time almost uncontrollably until he was weeping, coughing, and gasping for breath.

"I'm sorry," he said, struggling to catch his breath. "I'm sorry. Sometimes I'm just given the gift of mirth and I can't stop laughing. The Eastern Orthodox monks at Athos talk about the gift of tears. I get the gift of giggles. What a fool I am! But come now, let's drink some of this beer from Norcia and be serious. Why has dear Father Lawrence sent you to see me? Are you in some kind of trouble?"

So I told him about our three-week session with Father Lawrence, and his theory about the Way of the Wilderness Warrior, and how each one of us had been given someone to meet, and how I was assigned to him.

He listened carefully and nodded as he sipped his glass of beer. When I had finished, he waved his thin hand in front of his face and said, "Yes. Yes. The Way of the Wilderness Warrior. I like it. Alliteration I always like. I think he dreamed up the name himself, you know. Father Lawrence is like that. Underneath the Marine and policeman lies a poet. He got his ideas from a friend of mine, Dom Gregory Morgan, who is a monk at St. Bede's in Baltimore."

"Yes. He mentioned Dom Gregory."

"Uh huh. Yes. That's right. So Gregory, as you might have heard, once studied to be a scriptwriter for Hollywood. That was a big mistake, but God uses our mistakes for His glory. Gregory used this hero's quest thing to map out the spiritual journey. Not a bad idea. Quite creative, I suppose—but who needs creativity in the spiritual life? The spiritual life is much more like chopping wood than writing a poem. What you need to chop wood is a good axe, not a creative idea."

"So you think the whole Way of the Wilderness Warrior is stupid?"

The old monk had a glint in his eye. "I didn't say that. I'm simply saying that it's a good idea, but it has its limitations. It is a map, but there are many maps of the spiritual journey. I am a Benedictine. I follow the Lord in the way of St. Benedict. There are Franciscans and Dominicans, Norbertines, and Jesuits. They follow the Lord in the paths of their founders. Then there are the Carmelites. They have great masters: St. John of the Cross, St. Teresa of Ávila, dear little St. Thérèse of Lisieux. Then there is St. Francis de Sales and the other monastic masters: Sts. John Cassian, Basil, Pachomius, and the other Desert Fathers. The Russians too. Maps. They all have maps, guides, seven levels of the crystal castle, stairways to Heaven—you name it. All of them are worthwhile. All of them are worthless."

I frowned and took a deep gulp of beer. "I don't get it. Why worthless?"

"Have you ever been to London?"

"No."

"When you go to London, you will need a map. I suppose they don't have them anymore, because people have maps on their phones that connect with satellites, but back in the day, you were given this big book, *London A–Z*, which was a detailed street map of the city. That was all well and good if you were on foot or in a car, but there were also maps of the different city bus routes, and a famous map of the underground train system, which they call 'the Tube.' The three maps looked completely different, but they were maps of the same territory. So it is with the different forms of spirituality. They cover the same territory but look very different. If you were to compare the three maps in London, you would find points of congruence. St. Paul's Cathedral, for example, would appear on all three maps, because it's a famous landmark. It would not only be on the street map, but buses and tube trains would stop there. St. Paul's gave its name to a part of the city, so that section would also be named and marked on all the maps. So it is with the Way of the Wilderness Warrior. It is a map of the spiritual journey that overlaps and connects with the other ways."

"That makes sense."

"So here is what I propose," he said, after swallowing a huge gulp of Benedictine beer. "How long will you be here?"

"I can stay here for about two or three months."

"That's plenty of time. We'll meet every day for a week or so— however long it takes. In the meantime, enjoy your time at Cripple Creek. Join in with the life of the monks the best you can. Brother Boniface will help you. If you wish, I will walk you through the rest of Father Lawrence's way, and we'll see where it leads us. Does that sound like a good idea?"

"Sure."

"Good. Now, let me scratch your back."

"I'm sorry? What do you mean?"

That giggle again. "Don't be alarmed. It's monastic slang for making your confession. How long has it been since your last confession?"

I blushed. "I don't know, maybe a month or two?"

He frowned. "You don't know? That's not good. If you are to learn about the spiritual way, then Confession is at the heart of it, because humility is at the heart of it. Confession is the practical application of repentance, and you know what repentance is, don't you?"

"Doing an action to make up for your sin?"

"That's penance. Often confused with repentance. The Greek word in the New Testament for 'repentance' is *metanoia*, which means 'turning around.'"

At this point, the mad monk got up and turned toward the fireplace. Then he spun around unsteadily to look at the opposite wall, where his oratory stood. "Turn from the fire and look to the purifier!" Then he started doing a little dance, turning round and round while singing, "Round and round and round we go, and where we stop, the Lord only knows."

Then he collapsed, coughing and breathless, back into his chair. He reached over and took my two hands in his and looked into my eyes and into my soul. "Repentance," he said, "is not just saying you're sorry for the naughty things you've done. Repentance is saying you're sorry for *sin* — the sin of the whole world. Repentance is not a thing you do. It is a truth you live. You must ask not only for *metanoia*, but for the *metanoia* mentality. Someone asked the old monk what they do in the monastery all day, and do you know what he answered?"

"Tell me."

He laughed and said, "We fall down, and we get up again. We fall down, and we get up again. Repentance is a state of mind, and a state of life. Do you understand?"

"I think so."

"I said there are many ways. One of the dearest, freshest deep-down things is a little book called *The Way of the Pilgrim*. It's from

Russia—the dear, passionate Russians! So much suffering! In this little book, a man goes on a pilgrimage to find the answer—much as you are—and do you know what the question is?"

"No, what's the question?"

"The question is: 'How can I learn to pray without ceasing?' You know this verse from the Bible about praying without ceasing?"

"No."

"You are a beginner."

"Yes, but I'd like to know."

He hurried to the big desk, pushed some books and papers aside, and stumbled back over to his seat with a big black Bible. "First Thessalonians, chapter 5. Listen to this: 'Rejoice always. Pray without ceasing. In all circumstances give thanks, for this is the will of God for you in Christ Jesus' (16-18)." He slammed the book closed and looked at me, with fire burning in his pale blue eyes. "Every day you pray the Our Father, and you pray to God, 'Thy will be done.' Right?"

"Right."

He tapped the book and said, "And here, St. Paul says what God's will is. *This* is the will of God for you: Rejoice always. Pray without ceasing. Give thanks in all circumstances. So this Russian man set out on a pilgrimage to discover how to pray without ceasing, and he eventually discovers the *hesychasm*. This is a way of contemplation centered on the Jesus prayer. It is prayer that is repeated over and over—linking it with your breathing—until it lodges in the very core of the person. Quite brilliant, when you think about it. What is the thing you do without ceasing?"

"Think?"

"Yes, but more basic. You breathe. So, to rejoice always and pray without ceasing, you link your rejoicing to your breathing. Breathe in," and here he took a deep breath, "and you say 'The

Lord our God is good.' Breathe out," and here he exhaled loud and long and said, " 'And His mercy endures forever.' John Cassian recommended that when you are tempted, you breathe in, saying, 'O God, come to my assistance" and breathe out with 'O Lord, make haste to help me.' That way, you pray without ceasing. Our Holy Father St. Benedict read Cassian." Here he waved his bony hands again and said, "You'll find it all in the Rule. Now, that Russian said the prayer should be. . . ." and he closed his eyes and said, "Breathe in: Lord Jesus Christ, Son of the Living God," and he paused, then exhaled as he finished, "have mercy on me, a sinner."

He opened his eyes, and I saw they were glittering with enthusiasm. "You see? Simple. Simple, but not easy. This prayer contains repentance and faith. Repentance in the plea for mercy. Faith in the trust placed in the Lord Jesus for forgiveness. So no matter which path you follow—Carmelite, Franciscan, Salesian, Ignatian, Benedictine, Thérèsian, or even that of the Russian Orthodox hermits—repentance is the first step, and it is the first step of every step. We begin, continue, and end with repentance."

Then he smiled at me in a way that pierced my heart. His eyes were full of a radiance and warmth that I had never seen before. His smile was one of acceptance and compassion and hilarity with a touch of craziness all rolled together. He said, "So would you like to make a good confession?"

For some reason I was suddenly overwhelmed with emotion. My lip began to tremble. He took my hands and said, "It will be all right. God looks on us with pity, not with blame. If you like, I will ask you some questions to help you examine your conscience. Dear brother, would you like me to do so?"

"Yes, please."

So I began with making a good confession, and that's when the journey really started.

9

The Step of Faith

Father Aelred got up and crossed to his little oratory and gestured for me to follow. He took the straight chair from behind the table and waved his hand toward the prayer desk facing the crucifix. I knelt as he placed the chair next to me. I crossed myself and began, "Bless me, Father, for I have sinned. My last confession was six months ago."

"May the Lord be in your heart and on your lips that you might make a good confession," he responded. And then, "You told me a moment ago that it'd been two months. Which is it?"

"Six months."

"You must never lie to me again."

"Sorry, Father."

"Promise? If you lie to me, I can do nothing for you. Promise?"

"Promise."

"Good. Now, before you begin, I wish to remind you of the seven capital sins. We will use them as the structure for your confession. As we go through them, I want you also to pay attention to the one that is your besetting sin, or your dominant sin. For most people, there's a biggie. These seven sins were outlined by the Church Fathers, and they still hold up pretty well. Maybe you know them already?"

"Remind me?"

"Of course. The first is pride—the root of all sin. This is not the proper pride in accomplishments well done, but rather the underlying mindset that you know it all—that you will do things your way, that it is your will that comes first. Are you guilty of pride?"

"Yes, Father. I want my own way all the time, in a bunch of different ways."

"It's good for you to recognize this. Remember that pride is also the most deeply rooted of sins. It is cured only through humility, and humility is endless, and endlessly mysterious."

"Why mysterious, Father?"

"Because if you believe you have achieved it, you most certainly have not, and when you have by God's grace achieved it, you will believe you have not."

"I see. Or, at least, I think I do."

"The next is envy. Envy is not only desiring the possessions or gifts of another person but wishing evil against that person for having them. Envy leads to resentment and revenge and ultimately violence if left unchecked because the envious will eventually take what they want and kill the other person to get it, if necessary. Cain was envious of his brother Abel, and that was the introduction of murder into our world. Have you been envious?"

"I don't think so. If anything, I've looked down on people with more and better stuff than I have."

"You come from a poor family, correct?"

"Yes, Father."

"Sometimes the poor deny their envy by telling themselves they are better than the rich. Reverse envy is a twisted form of envy."

"This is getting complicated."

"Sin *is* complicated—virtue is simple. This is because sin is always a virtue that is twisted. Evil is the distortion or destruction of goodness, truth, and beauty. The devil cannot create anything.

He can only twist or kill what is good. Now, moving on: the third deadly sin is anger, or wrath." He paused. "Anger. There is nothing wrong with anger as such. It is an emotion, and we are not culpable for our emotions. However, we are responsible for our reactions to our emotions. Wrath is anger that is nurtured and develops into rage, resentment, and revenge. Are you guilty of wrath?"

"No. I usually let things slide. It's not worth getting angry."

"I see. Well, that brings us to the next capital sin, which is sloth. Sloth is an unwillingness to get involved. Wrath is a hammer. Sloth is a hammock. Sloth can lead to despair and depression. Do you plead guilty or not guilty?

"Guilty. Big time. I get depressed sometimes—*really* depressed." I paused to gather myself because admitting my depression brought tears to my eyes again. "I'm sorry, Father. I don't know why I keep crying."

"Tears are a gift. Don't be ashamed. Why do you get depressed?"

"I don't know. I guess sometimes I'm just lonely."

"There are some people who suffer from clinical depression. This is complicated, and some think it is a chemical condition. However, many others suffer from a deep sadness and call it depression. They have denied and suppressed their anger, and it emerges as sadness. They come to think life is not worth living when they're sad, but it was giving in to sloth that stopped them from living and led to their sadness in the first place. What they called depression was the symptom, not the cause."

"How do I snap out of it?" I sniffed.

"Stop crying to start with." And suddenly Looney Tunes sounded stern. "People who suffer from sloth are usually sorry for themselves. Stop feeling sorry for yourself, recognize your anger, and confess the sin of sloth."

"Okay," I said, and I wiped my nose with my sleeve. "I confess the sin of sloth. What's next?"

"Avarice. Also known as greed. This is the disproportionate or disordered love of money or possessions."

"I really don't think I'm guilty of that, Father."

"Why not?"

"Well, my family is poor, but I think they gave me the right values on that one. Dad gives 10 percent of his income to the Church and tells us that money won't make us happy."

"That's good. I believe you. You are blessed to have that foundation. Many do not. Gluttony is the sixth sin, and it is linked to avarice. It is a disproportionate or disordered desire for food or drink. How do you plead? Guilty or not guilty?"

"A little bit guilty. I've overeaten, and I've also gotten drunk sometimes."

"Drugs?"

"I've smoked a little weed—only a little, when I was feeling depressed."

"Did it help?

"No. In the long run, I only got more depressed. Same thing with getting drunk."

"So you learned your lesson."

"I think so."

"Good. Now ... saving the worst for last. Lust."

"Yeah.... No description needed, Father. Guilty."

"Male or female?"

"What?"

"Are your desires for men or women?"

"I. Uh ..."

"Don't lie. You promised."

"Uh. Well ... to be perfectly honest ... it's both, Father."

"I never believe people when they preface their remark with 'to be perfectly honest.' So, which is it? Men or women?"

I really broke open at that point. "I guess it's mostly other men, Father." And I sobbed.

"Just as I thought," he said. "And are you guilty of lustful actions with other men or lust in your heart and mind?"

"I've been with a girl and had one or two relationships with other guys, but mostly porn and masturbation."

"Did you commit sodomy with the other men?"

"No, Father."

"I believe you. Thank you for making a good confession. Now, which of the seven do you feel is your besetting sin? Which one is the root of the others?"

"Probably lust, Father."

"Yes. We'll talk more about that later. In the meantime, for your penance, I would like you to memorize Psalm 103. Can you do this?"

"Memorize it?"

"Yes. In the King James Version. It is easier to memorize, and the language is more beautiful. Do this for our next meeting."

"Got it." I began to get up.

"Hold on. First make your Act of Contrition; then I will grant your absolution."

So I did, and he did, and we got up and returned to the chairs in front of the fire.

He shooed Jeoffrey from his chair again and sat down, smiling at me.

"Feeling better?"

"Yes, Father. Thank you."

"I can see we have some work to do, but Rome wasn't built in a day. Brother Boniface will be back to pick you up in an hour or so. Until then, shall we get some lunch?"

"Sure."

He headed for the little kitchen corner, rummaged in a cupboard, and brought out a can of chicken noodle soup. He also found a loaf of homemade bread and a big block of cheese.

"The Collins family live up the road," he said, patting the bread. They've moved here from Oregon to be near the monastery. He works in computers, and she homeschools their eight kids. Lucky for me, part of their morning regime is to bake half a dozen loaves of bread, and one of the kids rides over on their trail bike twice a week to bring me one. The Norbertine nuns in California make the cheese. They have it delivered to the monastery, and Brother Philip, the cellarer, always sends me a chunk—so, soup, bread, and cheese it is. It could be worse!"

We put our bowls of soup and a cutting board with the bread and cheese on a corner of the big table. He brought the chair he had used for Confession back to the table and then reached behind the curtain of his bedroom corner and brought out a folding chair.

Over lunch, Father Aelred said, "Austin, you should understand that what Father Lawrence wants me to share with you is really only an outline of what is to come. If you are seeking the perfection that is your destiny, all I can do is point the way and tell you what to expect. The map is not the journey. The journey itself will take a lifetime. It takes a lifetime to learn how to love. That's why marriage vows—and monastic vows—are for life."

"Okay," I said, "and I hear what you're saying about the different paths, but I'm getting confused about Father Lawrence's Way of the Wilderness Warrior. Where does it all fit in?"

Father Aelred stood up and cut a thick slice of bread and a wedge of cheese, then handed them to me on a plate. "Let's start back at the beginning," he said. "The first five stages of his way are: First, the Ordinary World. Second, Hearing the Call. Third …"

"Refusing the Call. We all remember that."

"Good. Fourth—Meeting the Mentor. I guess that's me," he said and laughed that oddly unsettling, high-pitched chuckle again. "You got Looney Tunes for your mentor. Sorry about that! Now, the fifth stage is The Turning, which you have just learned about and experienced in making a good confession."

"But you said that stage needs to be a permanent condition."

"Correct. In fact, all of the stages are a permanent condition. We're always going through these steps until we get to the sixth stage, which Father Lawrence and Father Gregory call the Step of Faith. These first six stages overlap with what some of the spiritual masters call the Purgative Stage."

"What's that?"

"Classic Catholic spirituality thinks of three stages on the path to perfection—the Purgative, the Illuminative, and the Unitive. The first is getting rid of all the bad stuff. The second is building up all the good stuff. The third is living in true union with Christ."

"That sounds pretty intense."

"Oh, believe me. It gets very intense, and very technical. If you want to get a taste of just how technical it gets, have a look at this." He got up from the table, crossed over to the bookshelves, squinted at the titles for a few moments, pulled out a thick volume, and came back and handed it to me. "Here. Take this along for some bedtime reading."

The book was an old hardbound volume of about five hundred pages of close print. It was titled *The Three Ages of the Interior Life*.

I flipped through it and sampled a page at random, reading without speaking:

If acquired faith, born of the historical examination of the gospel and of the miracles that confirm it, were sufficient to attain the formal motive of the Christian faith, infused faith should be useless, as would infused hope and infused charity. Natural good will, spoken of by the Pelagians, would suffice. In the opinion of the Pelagians, grace and the infused virtues were not absolutely necessary for salvation, but only for the easier accomplishment of the Christian life.

"Whew!" I said. "Five hundred pages of that? Bedtime reading for sure. It'll cure any insomnia I might have."

Father Aelred chuckled and waved his hand. "I've never had much use for that book. It's too dry. I'm sure it's all very worthwhile, but poor old Garrigou-Lagrange makes the spiritual life a matter of mechanical technicalities. Some people love him. I think it's too much like hard work. It reminds me of those old manuals for confessors who had to advise married people about sin."

"What do you mean?"

"You should read them sometime," Father Aelred laughed. "They would say things like, 'If the man should touch his sacred spouse between the elbow and the shoulder he does not sin. However, should his hand stray above the shoulder toward the breast in such a way as to cause arousal in himself or his sacred spouse, and should they not continue to coitus that is fully open to life, then both are guilty of a mortal sin.'"

I spluttered on my soup. "You're kidding me!"

"I am exaggerating a bit, I suppose, but my point is that this approach to either loving your wife or loving the Lord can become too dry, too technical, too legalistic. Love is never legalistic. There are rules to love, but no laws."

"You lost me there."

He waved his hand again. "Never mind. We can discuss it all later. The Purgative Stage is where we all start, but the Carmelites give the impression that you can move on, that it is something you progress out of. I think that is possible, but it is more likely that most of us continue in the Purgative Stage and, instead of moving entirely out of one stage into another, we add a new stage to it. Earlier writers speak of the purgation being a fixed reality. St. John Cassian talks about three renunciations. The first is the renunciation of our physical pleasures and attachment to our possessions. The second is our renunciation of what Father Lawrence calls our Ordinary World. The third is the attraction to the good, the beautiful, and the true. The classic Carmelite way sees the first two as the Purgative Stage and the third as the Illuminative Stage."

"You're losing me here, Father. Too deep, too soon."

He laughed and waved his hand again. "Of course. I'm sorry. You're right. And that's what I mean about this all getting too technical—like Garrigou-Lagrange. It's not bad, of course, but let's not run before we walk. By the way, while you're here, you also really need to read the *Rule of St. Benedict*. Somehow or other, he gathers up all of this spirituality in his own way, which has always been the best way for me. I expect the monks will tell you about it in time."

We finished our lunch, and he handed me an apple. "Come on. Let me show you my garden."

We wandered outside and stopped where he had been splitting logs. He pointed out where he was growing vegetables and showed me the netting over his strawberry plants and his berry bushes and the clutch of fruit trees at the far end of the enclosure.

"I'm getting a hive of bees in the spring," he said. "Brother Martin is bringing one down from the monastery. They'll help pollinate the fruit trees, and of course we get honey, and then the wax for the candles. The monks make all the candles for Mass because the rules for the traditional Latin Mass stipulate beeswax. Don't ask me why, when those modern, oil-filled candles will do.

Call us Luddites, I guess." We paused for a moment, and I began to soak up the austere beauty of Father Aelred's life. The winter sun blazed through the bare trees as a gust of wind swept across the hills and into the little valley.

"I'm cold," he said suddenly, and he started to cough. "Let's go back inside."

After we were settled back in the armchairs, he said, "What I did want to say before you go is that this step of the Turning is linked with the fifth stage, which is the Step of Faith. You must get hold of this before Brother Boniface comes to pick you up."

"Okay, I'm listening," I said, as I bit into a chunk of bread and cheese.

"People are very mixed up about faith—and that is all the fault of that stinker Martin Luther."

"Did you say 'thinker,' Father?" I asked, not sure if I should laugh.

"No. Stinker. Martin Luther gave us the idea that faith was all about a person's individual response to God's truth. So the more emotional folks began to think faith was a personal, emotional experience. They had 'faith' because they were perhaps ashamed, or felt sad and sorry for their sins, and accepted Jesus into their heart because a preacher told them that would make them feel better—or more likely that it would give them a ticket to Heaven. Then, when the emotion died away, they considered faith the thing they did when they were trying very hard to believe something that they knew, deep down, was a load of hogwash. None of this is faith."

"So what is faith?"

"The Bible tells us exactly what faith is." He reached for the Bible, turned to Hebrews, and read from the beginning of chapter 11: "Faith is the substance of things hoped for, the evidence of things not seen" (see v. 1, KJV).

"I've heard that before but never understood it."

"And you say you're a philosophy major? You're right, the verse is a bit of a riddle—especially since Luther confused everybody about faith. The key to the riddle is the word 'substance.' What does that mean in medieval philosophy? Do you remember?"

"It does not mean something physical. It refers to the invisible realities—the inner quality of a thing that is eternal and objective and therefore real."

"Yes. Thus, the philosophers who held this belief were called realists. And what is transubstantiation?"

"It is the transformation of the substance of the bread and wine into the Body and Blood of Christ. The substance being the inner, invisible, objective quality of the bread and wine."

"Excellent!" His blue eyes shone with enthusiasm. "So faith is the solid, objective, eternal, but invisible reality of things hoped for. What is hoped for?"

"Happiness? Eternal life? Salvation? Perfection?"

"All of the above. And the writer of Hebrews is saying that faith is the solid evidence of this invisible hope. Faith is not simply an emotion, nor is it an intellectual effort to believe a doctrinal proposition. Faith may produce an emotion, as a cold may produce a sneeze, but faith is not that emotion. Faith is the reality of God incarnate. It is Mary's Son—the Son of Man and Son of God, objective in history. It is the Church—the sacrament of salvation—the Body of Christ objective in history. This is why we call Catholicism 'the Faith.' Individual faith is a life lived intentionally within and as part of this objective, historical reality."

He coughed again briefly, paused for a drink, and then continued. "The stage of the journey that comes along with the Turning is the Step of Faith. This is not some irrational, emotional foolhardy decision. It is a logical and real acknowledgment of the truth of the Gospel and a life that is lived within this truth. Do you see?"

I was amazed at his explanation. I had never seen it like that. "I do see. The faith is my decision to live this life and pursue this promise."

"You got it." He stood up again and walked to the fireplace and faced it. Then, once again, he turned rapidly to the other side of the room, to the crucifix, and he said, "Turn from the fire to the purifier. These two stages—the Turning and the Step of Faith—go hand in hand. Will you do this?"

I was confused for a moment and looked at him, questioning. He gestured for me to join him as he stood facing the fire, and I realized what he wanted. I got up a little sheepishly and stood next to him but said, "This is kind of silly."

"I know," he laughed. "Forgive me. This is how I earned my name. But join me."

So I also faced the fire, then turned and said, "Turn from the fire to the purifier."

As I did, something amazing happened. As I stood and gazed at the silver crucifix, it seemed that there was blood flowing from His hands, feet, and side. His whole body seemed bathed in blood, and, as I watched, my eyes began to fill again, and it seemed that Christ lifted His head from the Cross, and I swear He looked straight at me.

I stood there transfixed for what seemed ages. Jesus' gaze grew stronger and pierced me to the heart. Then I collapsed in a faint, and Father Aelred caught me.

10

Friends, Allies, and Enemies

I found myself lying on my back, on the floor by the fire, with my head cradled in Father Aelred's arm. I opened my eyes and saw his face—pale blue eyes and rosy cheeks. At first, he was alarmed; then I saw a quiet confidence return to his face as he realized I was coming to.

"Here," he said, reaching to the little table between the chairs, "drink this. It's Calvados."

"What's Calvados?" I asked, as I sipped from the tiny glass.

"Apple brandy from Normandy—the area around Lisieux in France—the land of Thérèse. It will strengthen you. You've had a shock. What caused you to pass out?"

I sat up. "I don't know. I've been stressed out coming here. I'm tired."

"Maybe your confession was stressful. Did you confess something you've never discussed with anyone before?"

I nodded, "Yes, Father. But there's more than that. I had a vision of Christ crucified."

"Yes. You were gazing at the crucifix. It was your Turning and your Step of Faith."

I was alert now, remembering what I had seen. "But Christ's body was bathed in blood. His wounds were flowing, and He raised his head and looked at me." I shook my head. "I know it sounds crazy, but it was real!"

Father Aelred smiled and said, "Others have witnessed that and thought I had a miraculous crucifix in my oratory. But I think there is a more ordinary explanation. When the afternoon light is right through the front window, the flames from the fire are reflected in the silver plating of the Christ figure and it looks like He is either on fire or bathed in blood. If the fire flickers, the shadows play across the Lord's head, and it seems like His head moves. You were in a vulnerable state of mind, as you say, stressed and tired, and you perceived these very natural circumstances in the supernatural way you described."

"So, it wasn't real." I said. "It was just an illusion—a trick of light and shadows, smoke and mirrors."

"I didn't say that," Father Aelred replied. "I said what you experienced consisted more of what you perceived than what objectively occurred. That doesn't mean your perception of what happened was necessarily incorrect. An inconsistency between what is real and what we perceive to be real is very often the way miracles happen."

"What do you mean?"

"Well," he chuckled, "human perception is a mysterious thing. We think what we perceive with our physical senses is always a reliable source of truth. We say, 'I won't believe it unless I see it.' But very often, people do see things and yet still don't believe them. I had a woman here once who saw her dead husband appear to her every night at nine o'clock, drinking a cup of hot chocolate, but she didn't believe her eyes."

"So was it a miracle or not?" I demanded.

"Let's just say it was a powerful way the Lord used to touch you and communicate with you. How did your vision of the Lord bathed in blood make you feel?"

"I felt overwhelmed. I felt terrible about myself and how sinful I am, and I also felt how much He suffered for me ..."

"Is that all?"

"No," I paused, choked up. "I also felt—more than I can say—how much He loves me."

"And that's when you passed out?"

"Yes."

With that, there was a knock at the door, and Brother Boniface stepped in.

"Ready to go?" he asked.

We got up. Father Aelred put his arm around my shoulder and said to Brother Boniface, "We have had a good time getting to know each other." He looked at me and said, "Come again the day after tomorrow after lunch. There is a path that comes here over the fields and fences from the abbey. It branches off about halfway down the main driveway. Brother Boniface can point it out on the way back. It will take about forty-five minutes to hike it."

I followed Brother Boniface across the brook and up the hill to the pickup truck, and as we bounced back over the rough road, he asked me, "So, what did you think of our hermit?"

"I like him," I said. "Why is there only one hermit?"

"In the Rule, St. Benedict says there are four types of monks: the Cenobites, the hermits, the gyrovagues, and the sarabaites. The Cenobites live in monasteries. The hermits are those who have lived in the monastery for a long time and come to feel called to the solitary life. Benedict says they are the front-line troops in the battle against the devil. Father Aelred is our main man; that little hermitage is a real battleground. Did you know he is also an exorcist?"

"No. Really?"

"Yes. There have been some mighty strange events reported from Father Aelred's little hut in the woods. Some people go there and are healed. Others, converted. Some have demons cast out. Some have visions."

"What kind of visions?"

"It depends on the person. Father Aelred has been seen to levitate when he's praying, and some people have even reported that he bilocates."

"What's that?"

"When people see him somewhere else, but we know he's really there in the hermitage praying."

"Who sees him?"

"Some of the monks have seen him praying in the abbey church at the same time we know he must be in the hermitage. One of the Collins kids said he came to see her when she was in the hospital for heart surgery, but he couldn't have been there because it was in Oklahoma City, and he couldn't have gotten there. Most of us aren't sure what to make of it, and when Aelred is asked about it, he just explains it away, says what we perceive is not always reliable."

"Does he usually explain the miracles away?"

"Sometimes he admits there are miracles in what he does, but he never makes a big deal out of it. Like, when he had the stigmata."

"What's the stigmata?"

"Supernatural wounds of Our Lord's Crucifixion appear on a person's body. St. Francis and Padre Pio and some other people had them."

"And Father Aelred has them?"

"Not now. Not always, and maybe never, but Brother Nicholas swears he saw blood on Father Aelred's head and hands on Good Friday last year."

As we drove through the gate onto the main driveway to the abbey, Brother Boniface looked in the rearview mirror and said, "There's Father Jacob!"

I looked out the rear window and saw a black Chevy Malibu following us. As we pulled into the parking lot, it pulled in beside us, and a tall, handsome, middle-aged monk got out. He had dark hair with graying temples, dark eyes, and a broad smile.

"Boniface!" he called out and gave Brother Boniface a huge hug. Boniface stepped back and said, "This is Austin. He's visiting for a few weeks."

"Thinking of becoming a monk?" Jacob said. "Don't do it! Look what it's done to Boniface!" And he poked Boniface's pudgy belly.

Boniface rolled his eyes and gestured toward the church. "It will be time for Vespers in about a half hour," he said. "Jacob, are you going to join us?"

Father Jacob said, "I have to catch up on some correspondence. I'll see you after dinner."

As we walked to the church, Brother Boniface told me, "Father Abbot has said you should spend the work time tomorrow back on the fence crew with Matthew, James, and Nicholas."

By the next morning, I found I was already getting used to the monastic routine. It seemed natural and wholesome. The food was simple but plentiful and good, and although I had thought that all the liturgical time in church would become boring, I was instead finding it refreshing just to sit in the vast space of the church and allow the Gregorian chant to take me into a place of stillness and calm.

That day I worked with the three brothers, digging holes for the fence posts and laying out what seemed like miles of barbed wire around the perimeter of one of the pastures. We got to talking as we worked. James was older than the other two, and it turned out that Matthew and Nicholas had come to the monastery at about the same time.

Nicholas said, "I was a sophomore in college, trying for an engineering degree, when I decided to drop out. I hated engineering, but I loved working with my hands and being outside. When I came here for a visit, I knew immediately that this is where I wanted to spend my life."

"What about you, Matthew?" I asked.

"I came here from Canada," he said. "I tried to be a monk at a monastery up there, but the monks were all old and weary. The place was dead." He gripped Nicholas on the shoulder and his eyes gleamed. "But I've got brothers my own age here, and we're good friends. Right, mate?"

Nicholas beamed. "Right! You gotta have brothers-in-arms in this battle."

"So," I started, curious to get their feedback on a few things, "I spent most of yesterday with Father Aelred."

Matthew laughed, "I'll bet that shook you up, eh?"

"Yes," I nodded. "A little, for sure."

"Most of us go down there for Confession," said Nicholas. "It doesn't do any harm for him to shake you up."

"Do you guys believe the stories about him bilocating and the stigmata?" I asked.

"Sure," replied Matthew.

"Why not?" shrugged Nicholas, and then he winced as he caught a bare forearm on a coil of the barbed wire. "Okay, time to focus on this. Back to work!"

My back was aching by the time we trudged back to the abbey for Vespers late that afternoon.

Dinner sure tasted good after all that manual labor. After dinner, I fell asleep right away and woke up at only nine o'clock when the bell rang for Compline.

Compline is a beautiful combination of psalms asking for God's protection through the night. It concludes with a hymn to Mary. That night, it was the "Alma Redemptoris Mater." After Compline is what the monks call the Great Silence. No one is to speak or visit until the morning bell.

I crept back to my room and read the *Rule of St. Benedict* for fifteen minutes. I was surprised that it was just simple rules for life in a monastery. I was expecting a detailed instruction manual on the spiritual life. Benedict weaves his teaching on prayer into the daily routine. It was practical and down to earth. I liked that.

Feeling drowsy, I put the book down and was just getting undressed for bed when there was a knock on my door. Without my shirt on, I opened the door to find Father Jacob standing there. He looked me up and down and smiled.

"I'm sorry to interrupt you, but I like to get to know the visitors. Can I come in?"

"Sure," I said and pulled on my T-shirt.

He pulled out the chair from the desk and sat down. I took the armchair.

"So, you're one of Lawrence Roper's protégées, are you?"

"I guess so. Do you know Father Lawrence?"

"I've heard about him. I have some friends at St. Bede's in Baltimore."

"I guess he's pretty well known."

"Yes, in certain circles. So, Austin, what brings you to Cripple Creek?" he asked.

"I was told to come meet Father Aelred."

He chuckled. "Dear old Aelred," he said. "You know why they call him Looney Tunes, don't you?"

"Just a joke about his name, I guess."

"Maybe I shouldn't tell you this, but he's had a couple of spells of treatment for mental illness. Clinical depression, and I think paranoia. It's sad. I think Father Abbot was quite relieved when Aelred asked to build a hermitage."

"He didn't seem crazy to me. Maybe eccentric, but not really crazy."

Father Jacob squinted at me and said, "Have you ever met anyone who was truly crazy?"

"No. I guess I haven't."

"Well, I can tell you, they hardly ever seem crazy at first. It's only when you get to know them that you realize they're not really in touch with reality. Now tell me," he leaned closer, "did Aelred search you about your 'besetting sin,' as he calls it?"

"He did." Father Jacob was making me feel uncomfortable.

"You can tell me." He smiled. "I'm a priest. It is the seal of the confessional."

I wished I hadn't, but I went ahead and told Father Jacob about my confession—about the confession that I was guilty of lust and that I'd been with both guys and girls.

Father Jacob said, "That's not surprising, given the world we live in today. And did Father Aelred tell you how sinful you were?"

"Not really. He just listened and then gave me a penance and absolution."

"Uh huh. But he did not give you any counseling on the problem?"

"I think he said we would discuss it later."

Father Jacob got up and began to pace the floor slowly. As he did, he said, "Maybe I shouldn't tell you this, since I've only just met you, but Aelred is very old-fashioned. He'll tell you that your besetting sin—as he calls it—is something you need to be cured of, and that the only way to cure it is through a lifetime of prayer and self-denial."

"So what if he does?" I asked.

Father Jacob smiled again, and by now I was feeling chills down my back. There was something creepy about his smile and his manner. "Austin, Father Aelred's approach—like his hermit's life—is very old-fashioned. Some of us have learned a lot about the spiritual life through the new sciences, like psychology. We know more about human sexuality than in previous ages. If you have had some sexual experiences, I don't think there's so much harm in that. You're a young man. You're learning about love. As long as no one was harmed, what real problem is there with it?"

"But it's sinful, isn't it?"

"If you say so. But what is sin?"

"But it's not just me. The Church says it's sinful."

"According to rules that made sense two thousand years ago, in a very different culture. The Church adapts to the changing times and cultures. We don't deny that it is a sin, but we take a pastoral approach."

"What does that mean?"

"We meet you where you are, and listen to your circumstances, and try to understand your deepest needs. We accompany you and affirm you. Much of the Church's teaching in the past only led to unhealthy repression of a person's sexuality. It led to terrible self-esteem problems and contributed to the sexual abuse crisis. Men who were sexually repressed and immature acted out with children."

"Are you saying I'm that way?" I asked.

"Of course not! But Aelred's way has led to those kinds of problems in the past. There is a new way—a way of affirmation, joy, and acceptance."

He could see I was confused.

"Come here," he said and put his arms out to me. Before I knew it, I was in his arms, and he was embracing me. "I understand," he said. "You feel alone and sad and guilty."

He released me, and I returned to the chair and watched him as he resumed pacing. He said, "There is no need to feel guilty for the way God made you. God doesn't make trash, you know. You were created good and created in God's image. Just remember that."

Then he came over, took my head in his hands, and gazed into my eyes. Then he kissed me. Not on the lips, but on the top of my head.

"Let me give you my blessing," he said, then he laid hands on my head. As he moved to leave the room, he turned and smiled at me. "We must talk more later."

11

The Point of No Return

I hardly slept that night, so I was glad to be relieved of work duty the next day. After lunch, instead of more hours building fences with Matthew, James, and Nicholas, I set out for Father Aelred's hermitage. The path was easy enough to find, and as I hiked across the frozen fields, I ran through in my mind what had happened the night before. Just who was this Father Jacob, and why did he come to my room? I had already been feeling pretty shaky after my first session with Father Aelred, disoriented with a new environment, new friends, new food, and a new routine. Father Jacob's visit felt like a step too far, in more ways than one. I was hoping Father Aelred might have some answers.

He was waiting for me by the fire. On the table were two more glasses of beer from Norcia and a bowl of popcorn.

"I thought you would want a snack after hiking over here," Father Aelred began. "The Collins kids love making popcorn, and they deliver a bag now and again with the bread. This batch has cheese on it."

As we each munched a handful, he said, "Cheesy popcorn. How do they do that?"

"I think you can get cheese in a powder, and you mix it in when the popcorn is still hot."

"I don't expect the Norbertine nuns in California make such delicious snacks, do you?"

"No idea," I said, as I sipped some beer.

"Today," Father Aelred said, "I want to review the Way of the Wilderness Warrior with you. After all, that is why Father Lawrence sent you here, isn't it? For a crash course in the spiritual path?"

I nodded and took another handful of popcorn.

"The first stage is the Ordinary World, then the Call to Adventure—the call to leave the Ordinary World—correct?"

"Yes. Father Lawrence explained those stages and went on to explain Refusing the Call and Meeting the Mentor. That's when he gave all nine of us a mentor to go meet. So, here I am."

"So here you are." Father Aelred smiled. "The day before yesterday, we met and discussed the next two stages: the Turning and the Step of Faith. You made your confession and then, before you left with Father Boniface, you had some sort of experience that caused you to pass out. Are you feeling better now?"

"I think so. Father Aelred, what do you make of that experience I had? It was so real. I can't believe it was just the reflection from the fire."

"You say it was real, but what is reality? If you are going on the spiritual path, then you are venturing into the invisible realm—the ultimate reality. It is like going into another country—no, more than that—like visiting another planet, where your usual modes of perception don't function."

"What do you mean?"

"When I was your age, I went to France with a few of my college friends, and we joined a French monastery. We had only recently become Catholics. We had just graduated from college, so facing the adult world in itself was stressful. Added to that, we didn't know French and had never spent a long time away from home. It was totally disorienting. Everything was different: food, language, routines, clothing, climate, politics, religion, everything. To tread in the spiritual realm is to enter a different world. That's why leaving the Ordinary World is so important and why Father Lawrence invited the nine of you to set out on a physical journey that would also be a spiritual adventure. The adventure in the physical realm prepares you for the adjustments that are necessary to enter the spiritual realm. It's there in the Rule. Our Holy Father Benedict says the young monk must learn instant obedience in the monastery to Father Abbot, so that when his Heavenly Father calls, he will already be trained in obedience.

"Whom to obey? This is the question, and discovering the answer requires discernment. St. John Cassian teaches that there are four kinds of discernment necessary. I'll get to that shortly, but first, you may remember that I said the first six stages of the Way of the Wilderness Warrior are like the Purgative Stage. After that, you enter the adventure proper—what the masters call the Illuminative Stage.

"The seventh step—and the first in the Illuminative Stage—is called Friends, Allies, and Enemies. Once he has taken the Step of Faith into the World of Adventure, the hero encounters new friends—others who have also left the Ordinary World to embark on the adventure. This is a joyful thing, but there is a problem."

"What's that?"

"The enemies are also encountered, and the whole matter is complicated by the fact that the enemy often appears to be a friend. This is where Cassian's wisdom about discernment comes into play.

"Cassian uses the analogy of money to explain the four kinds of discernment. In ancient times, money—the coins themselves, that is—were made of genuine precious metals; they were not paper bills such as we use today. The coins were actually gold or silver. They were worth something in and of themselves. A coin could be made of some cheaper metal, such as bronze or copper, and that's Cassian's first test. The coin could be made of real precious metal but be a counterfeit—that's the second test. The third is that the coin could bear a false image. Instead of the rightful king or emperor, it might bear an untrue image, thus reducing its authority and value. The fourth test is that the coin could be underweight and therefore have an insufficient value. People would grind a coin down and keep the shavings, or they'd cut a nick out of the coin to try the quality of the metal. We can use these four tests as a model in helping to discern the right path, or to discern the authenticity of teaching, or the authenticity of other people."

"I think I get it," I said. "When dealing with people, you could ask whether their credentials are bona fide or bogus. That's like asking whether the coin is made of gold or just cheap brass."

"Good. Yes," Father Aelred said.

"Then you could ask whether the person is a fake—a counterfeit."

"In the spiritual life, whether he is a hypocrite."

"The third test is whether the person bears a false image. What's that about?"

"What is the image that every baptized person should bear?"

"The image of Christ, I guess."

"Correct. A hypocrite—a bogus Christian—does not bear the image of Christ. He works under the authority of someone other than Christ. Likewise, a heretical teaching does not bear the image of the Gospel. It does not ring true to the whole teaching of the Catholic Faith. To discern the counterfeits, of course, the expert must get to know the real thing as well as possible," Father Aelred smiled.

I nodded, "There's this movie I saw called *Catch Me If You Can*. It's about a counterfeiter who gets caught and then he ends up working for the FBI. They hired him to catch other counterfeiters; because he'd become such an expert in copying the real thing, he also became an expert in spotting the fakes."

"Perfect," grinned Father Aelred. "And what about the fourth type of discernment—when the coin is underweight?"

"I guess that would be if the person or the teaching was kind of lightweight—maybe too easy?"

"Yes, too easy, and too sweet to the taste. False teachers always sentimentalize the Gospel and water it down. God's mercy is a severe mercy. Aslan is not a tame lion."

"Father Aelred," I asked, and then paused, a little uncertain. "Can I ask you about someone at the monastery?"

"Of course. We have no secrets."

"One of the monks. Father Jacob."

Aelred shook his head, "Oh dear. Is he back?"

"He arrived just as Boniface and I were returning from my first visit." Then, with some hesitation, but glad to get it off my chest, I told him about his visit to my room that night.

Father Aelred smiled sadly and said, "Jacob has not been good for our community, but, in a way, I'm glad he has returned. He is what our holy father St. Benedict called a 'gyrovague.'"

"Brother Boniface was telling me about the four kinds of monks. That was one of them, I think."

"Yes," said Father Aelred. "The gyrovague is a monk who drifts from region to region, never staying in one place. Benedict says their god is their appetite and they serve only themselves. They never settle down. They have no *stabilitas*, and are worse than the sarabaites."

"*Stabilitas*? Sarabaites?"

"*Stabilitas*: Stability. It is one of the vows a Benedictine takes, along with Obedience and Conversion of Life." He smiled, "More about that later perhaps."

"What are the sarabaites? It sounds like a fast-food snack."

Father Aelred laughed his odd, high-pitched chuckle, then explained, "The sarabaites are monks who go off on their own to set up their own communities according to their own beliefs and desires."

"Do-it-yourself monks."

"That's right. They always know best! Or so they think. But I have found that when groups of Christians split off to do their own thing, they end up splitting again. It makes sense. A community of people who think it is okay to do their own thing is a group of people who will eventually argue and disagree with one another. It happens in the Church all the time."

"Didn't you and your friends do that when you left your monastery in France to come here?"

"No! No, we did not. We founded this monastery under obedience and guidance from our abbot in France. While we were excited to be part of this adventure, all of us admitted that we would rather have stayed in France. The food was better," he chuckled.

"What about Father Jacob? Did he split off like that?"

"Jacob tried his vocation here with us, but he was not accepted by the community. After he left, he developed his own media ministry—teaching, leading retreats, and preaching. He maintains links with the monasteries he visits and presents himself as a monk, but he is not a true monk. Why Father Abbot allows him to come here I have no idea."

"He said you were crazy."

"I am not surprised."

"Said you have been hospitalized with mental illness."

Father Aelred's face clouded over. "That is not untrue, but Austin, did you think I had ended up here as a monk and as a hermit, at my age, never having been through any sort of trials and troubles? Yes, I have been through a dark tunnel, but, by God's grace, I have come through to a place of peace and light."

He sat staring glumly into the fire for what seemed ages, then said, "In fact, Father Jacob is a perfect test for Cassian's four kinds of discernment. Is Jacob a true monk?"

"Not as far as I can make out."

"You are right. A true monk is under obedience and is a member of his community. Is he counterfeit—and is his teaching false? What did he say to you?"

"I told him about my confession to you, and he said my sins were not really sins because we know more about human sexuality now than we used to."

"What did you think about that?"

"It didn't sound right to me. Like the fourth test—it was underweight."

"Correct. It is a false twisting of the gospel. Overemphasizing compassion dilutes the power of true teaching. Jacob's teaching also goes against the third test because it does not bear the image of the master. It contradicts Scripture and the Magisterium of the Church, which teaches that sexual immorality is indeed objective and grave sin."

"So what will you do?" I asked.

"Should we tell him to go away?"

I nodded. "He gives me the creeps."

"I will have another word with Father Abbot, asking that Jacob be expelled and not permitted to stay here again. He's a false teacher. A wolf in sheep's clothing. But—let us leave him for now.

There are two other aspects to this stage of Friends, Allies, and Enemies that I need to remind you of. More beer?"

He poured the rest of the bottle into my glass and said, "First, you should read the treatise by my namesake, Aelred of Rievaulx. He was a Cistercian monk in England in the Middle Ages. He wrote a whole book, *Spiritual Friendship*."

"Spiritual friendship?"

"Yes. How to discern a true and worthy friendship. He drew on the Roman philosopher Cicero, who argues that friendship springs from a shared love of virtue. Aelred of Rievaulx points out that there are three types of friendship. The first is carnal and leads to lust and sexual immorality. The second is worldly and is pursued only for material gain."

"Networking."

"What?"

"Networking—making friends because of what they can do for you."

"I see. Yes. Exactly. But the third form is spiritual friendship, which is based in each person's rightful and just place with one another and with God—and it is that shared humility, if you like, on which true affection and friendship are based."

"Humility? In what way?"

"True humility is being exactly what God created you to be—no more and no less—and that is also perfection or wholeness. Simplicity. Humility. Unity. Here's a bit of homework. You've started to read the *Rule*, correct?

"Yes, Father."

"Good. Read chapter 7. There's also a good book on it by Dom Augustine Wetta. There's a copy in the library. You can ask Brother Andrew, the librarian, to help you find it. Humility makes you the kind of person others want to be with. Put simply, when we meet

people like that, we want to be their friend, and they make the
very best friends. These are the people you want to accompany
you on your journey."

"The other monks strike me as that kind of person."

"And Father Jacob?"

"I think he was wanting something from me."

Father Aelred raised his eyebrows, then frowned. "Indeed. But
let us leave him for now. The truest friends on this spiritual journey
are truly humble, but they are already on the other side."

"What do you mean?"

"The saints and angels. Do you have a patron saint? Do you
know your guardian angel?"

"Not really."

"As you progress on this journey, you will find your own friends
on the other side, just as you come across friends in ordinary
life—you'll meet them as you journey."

"What do you mean?"

"Well, as you travel through life, you come across friends
with whom you connect, and you realize they are good for you,
and you like being with them. In fact, in my experience, God
brings such people into one's life. It's the same with the saints.
Get a good dictionary of the saints. Follow the calendar, and get
to know them when their days come up. You'll soon find some
who attract you with their courage, their faith, their zeal—their
love for Our Lord and Our Lady. If you pray with them and to
them, they will pray for you and help you in the journey, more
than you can imagine."

"For real?"

Father Aelred's blue eyes lit up with bright fire. "Oh, certainly
for real! You may also, eventually, become more aware of the presence of your guardian angel. If you ask for the angel's help and

guidance and protection, that presence will become clearer to you. And while we're talking about friends and angels, don't forget the reality of the dark angels. What does St. Peter say? 'Be sober and vigilant. Your opponent the devil is prowling around like a roaring lion looking for someone to devour.' [1 Pet. 5:8]. Our Lord was tempted by Satan in the wilderness. Being a Wilderness Warrior means engaging with the same wild beast who still dwells in the desert. You will develop gifts of discernment not only of people but also of spirits. I know you have this capability because of your perception of the crucifix when we last met."

"I thought you said that was just a play of light and reflections."

"You said that. I said you were perceiving reality in a different way, and that is one of the qualities you need if you are going to go on the Way of the Wilderness Warrior."

"So, you think I'm cut out for it?"

He smiled. "Sure. Why not? Now, let's drink up and hike back to the abbey. I'll come with you. I want to talk to Father Abbot."

We set off across the brook and up the path to where there was a gate in the fence. From there, the path led across the broad, khaki-colored Oklahoma hillside.

As we hiked, Aelred said, "So, now you understand what to look for in the seventh stage, and I trust you'll keep your wits about you as you discern who your friends and allies are—and be on your guard when the inevitable enemy seeks an encounter. These abilities will be crucial as you move ahead to the eighth stage. Did Father Lawrence tell you what it is?"

"No. He was leaving that up to you."

"The eighth stage is the Point of No Return. The hero is well on his way. He's made some friends, identified some enemies, but now he comes to a moment of truth."

"What's that?"

"He realizes that this is not just a walk in the park. It is not a visit to a theme park, where he is going to have a fake adventure for the day. The quest has become serious. He realizes that he has burned his bridges. He's in this thing for good, and there is no turning back. Even if he wants to return to the Ordinary World, he suddenly realizes he can't. It's changed while he's been away, and most important, he realizes that *he* has changed. If he went back, he would not fit in with that world anymore."

"You guys must have gone through that when you went to France."

Father Aelred chuckled and said, "You bet we did! We would get together and talk about what we were going through. It was tough but exciting—trying to learn French, studying philosophy and theology and Latin, and learning about the monastic life. It was all very exciting for the first year or so. Then, one Christmas, Brother Thomas said he missed his family and wanted to go home to Kansas. We talked him out of it, but it made all of us realize that we had taken a step that was irreversible. We had passed the Point of No Return."

"Why is that such a big deal?"

"Because the hero realizes for the first time that this quest is not only real but it is going to change him for good. No turning back. Already, he is not the person he used to be, and, while this is exciting, it is also disturbing. There is a kind of death that has happened, and the hero has to go through a bereavement process. There are strong emotions that always go with bereavement—grief for what is lost, anger, blaming others, and a sense of being lost, not knowing who you are anymore—a sense of disorientation. The world you thought you knew has disappeared, and the person you thought you were is no longer."

"That's a good thing, right?"

Father Aelred stopped hiking and gazed up at the sky for a long time; then he looked at me with watery eyes and said, "It hurts. I still sometimes mourn for that Kansas farm boy who didn't know what he was getting himself in for."

"But no regrets?" I asked.

"Nope." He resolved, "No regrets!" Then he stomped off at a pace far faster than an old man should have been up to. He turned and waved for me to follow. "Let's go!" he cried. "Further up and further in!"

As we approached the brow of the hill, we could see the monastery buildings nestled in the gentle valley below. The yellow brick was golden in the afternoon sun, and suddenly I felt a great surge of desire. This was what I wanted. This was the life I could live. I was excited as I thought, "People do this. They decide to be monks. They spend their lives here in this place with their brothers, seeking God together. I want this."

Aelred turned around, and I realized he was watching me. "While you are here for these few months," he said, "you will make a decision. It will take you on a long journey, and what I am teaching you is just giving you the map for your quest. Remember, this map is presented as step-by-step stages in the journey, but each stage is present in all the other stages, and each stage has to be lived over and over again. Entering into the journey also teaches one about the nature of time."

"I don't follow."

"Because we are mortals, we think of time as linear. Because we have a beginning and an end, we think all time must have a beginning and an end. Pagan and primitive cultures often see time as cyclical—the cycle repeats over and over again."

"The circle of life."

"Yes. In fact, both ideas of time are right. Time present and time past are both perhaps present in time future, and time future is present in time present and in time past. God sees the whole timeline as a present moment outside our notion of linear time. The stages of the journey are linear, but they are also cyclical. They are sequential, but they also repeat."

"So, there will be numerous Calls to Adventure?"

"Correct, and you will be asked numerous times, in different ways and in different circumstances, to leave an Ordinary World, to meet new mentors, turn and turn again, and to take steps of faith—some minor and some major—over and over again. The journey is therefore as much a cycle of life as it is a journey from A to Z. The liturgy reminds us of that."

"I don't follow."

"The liturgy is cyclical. The psalms in a pattern over and over again, the daily routine over and over again, the liturgical year—a cycle from Advent through Lent to Paschaltide, then, in the fall, it starts again. The cycle of life. The seasons of the heart."

I pondered what Father Aelred said, then gestured down toward the monastery in the valley below and said, "Do you think I will end up here?"

He laughed and squeezed my shoulder and said, "How do I know? I'm looney, remember? But now I hear the bell ringing for Vespers. Let's get ourselves down there and, in case I don't see you again this evening—don't open your door to strangers, and take another workday with Matthew, James, and Nicholas tomorrow. I'll see you the next day after lunch again. Does that work?"

"I'll see you then."

12

The Mother-Father Wound

The next day, two more of the lay brothers—Brother Peter and Brother Bartholomew—joined us on the fence-laying team. Brother Peter, a huge bodybuilder-type guy in his early thirties, was in charge of a tractor with a grader that was used to maintain the dirt roads. He was proud of his machinery and had offered to bring the tractor with the earth-auger attachment to make our lives easier—it could dig a hole for the fence posts in seconds. Bartholomew, whom the others called Bart, was short and stocky and had a shaved head and a shrewd, quiet way about him. We soon got a system going with Peter and Bart drilling and planting the posts, while Matthew, James, Nicholas, and I laid out the posts, measured and rolled out the wire, fixed it to the posts, and finished things off.

As we trudged back to the abbey for Vespers, a black car came speeding down the lane, churning up a cloud of tan dust. As he drove past us, I could see Father Jacob was furious.

"It looks like Father Jacob is not too happy," said Nicholas.

I saw Matthew and Bart exchange glances and nod to each other. They knew more than they were saying. I was learning that was the way with these monks. They didn't say much, and what they did say always seemed a bit guarded. So I said, "What's the story with Father Jacob?"

Matthew looked at Bart and Nicholas but said only "It's none of our business" and trudged on.

"I'll tell you," said Nicholas, but Matthew tugged at his sleeve, and Bart frowned and shook his head.

Finally, Bart said to me, "You have probably heard of the monastic vow of silence."

I nodded.

"Some monasteries have strict vows of silence. We don't. However, we take St. Benedict's Rule seriously, and he warns that idle words about others are a sin."

"I will set a guard on my ways, that I may not offend with my tongue," quoted Matthew.

"Okay. I get that," I said, "but Father Aelred has already told me a bit about Father Jacob."

"Did he come to your room after Compline?" Nicholas blurted out.

"Yes," I said.

"Did he ask about your sex life?" Bart asked.

"Yes."

"Did he, you know, make a pass at you?" Nicholas asked.

"Sort of."

The three of them nodded to each other; then Matthew said, "Father Jacob is a homosexual, and he claims to be celibate, but there are rumors about him—that he is a predator."

"Why is he allowed to come here?" I asked.

"We don't know," Matthew said. "I think Father Abbot doesn't want to give way to rumors, and maybe he thinks Father Jacob is redeemable. He likes to give everybody the benefit of the doubt, and he wants to save him from himself, so he lets him visit on very strict terms."

"Jacob looked pretty angry right now," said Nicholas. "Maybe Father Abbot has expelled him for good."

We got back to the abbey just in time to wash up and go to the church for Vespers. Afterward, I ate a hearty dinner with the monks. I was learning to enjoy meals without talking, as one of them read a book aloud. Then I went up to my room and read the *Rule of St. Benedict* after dinner. St. Benedict comes across as a wise, gentle, loving father. I read the chapter on humility and found I had mixed feelings. I didn't get why Benedict banned laughter, but I liked the part that said the monk will eventually get to the point where he does good because he actually *wants* that. At the beginning of the chapter, St. Benedict speaks about controlling our desires, and at the end, he says that by doing so, we end up desiring the right thing.

Before I knew it, the bell was ringing for Compline, and afterward I crashed and slept solidly until it was time to stumble down for Matins at six the next morning. Father Aelred had given me a short edition of the *Conferences of John Cassian*, so I spent the morning reading and looking forward to my next meeting with him. Cassian was more severe than Benedict and more detailed about the spiritual life. I found a good balance in reading the two of them almost side by side.

The midwestern winter had swept in with a vengeance. Brother Boniface lent me a hat and gloves, so I bundled up after lunch and hiked across the fields and down the little footpath to Aelred's hermitage. Smoke was rising from the chimney, so I knew he'd be ready by the fire. With any luck, he'd have a warm drink and a snack for me. And, in fact, when I came in, I smelled hot chocolate. Aelred laughed with delight as I came through the door.

"Look!" he said, as he gestured to the little round table. "The Collins kids brought me a box of cookies."

He handed me a mug of hot chocolate and the plate of oatmeal raisin cookies and said, "A hot, sweet drink for a hot, sweet topic: sex."

I gulped in surprise. I wasn't prepared for this and felt myself freeze up a little inside.

"Don't be alarmed," he said. "It's something that should be talked about freely without embarrassment, but that's rarely possible because we are talking about something so intimate and private. However, I think you can trust me, can't you?"

I nodded, "More than Father Jacob, I hope."

Father Aelred frowned, "I hope Abbot Leo followed my advice. He wants to help Father Jacob, but I said he has to go."

"I think we saw him go," and I told him how we'd seen Father Jacob speeding down the lane.

"It is not a tragedy," Father Aelred said. "He'll feel sorry for himself at first, but, in my experience, people like Father Jacob bounce back. The strength of their ego is inexhaustible." He paused, took a sip of hot chocolate, nibbled a cookie, and said, "Now then. Do you mind if we discuss sex?"

"I guess not."

"Good. It must be discussed, because our sexuality is such an integral part of who we are, and if we are to be transformed totally—which is, after all, the whole point of the spiritual journey—then this aspect of our lives must also be transformed. Let me start with a question."

He patted his chest and said, "Here we are in this physical world with these absurd bodies of flesh and bones, and body fluids, farts and sneezes, itches and urges, hair and crevices, wrinkles and orifices—and yet we are spiritual beings made for Heaven. It sometimes feels like we are half ape and half angel—what a wonder—what a mess! The Bible says we are fearfully and wonderfully made, but it forgot to add that the result is a messy contradiction—more like we are frightfully and weirdly made, and in the middle of the contradiction, like a symbol of it all, is this." And at this point, he patted his crotch. "Have you ever wondered why this is at the center of your body, at the bottom of your being?"

"No, not really."

"I mean, why not place the reproductive organs in the mouth, so that when a man and a woman kiss, they might reproduce? Why not in the hands or feet?"

I shrugged. It was a weird question, "I don't know."

"Our bodies reflect a beautiful, symbolic unity. The sexual organs are at the bottom of the belly, in the middle of our bodies, because sex is at the foundation and center of our being. This is at the center of the contradiction: this most powerful physical urge is also the organ through which we can cooperate with God in the creation of a new eternal soul. It is there at the center of our being, and the foundation of our bodies reminds us that each one of us was formed through a sexual encounter, a moment of sexual pleasure. That experience of our parents was the spark of our own life. Sex is therefore at the very foundation level of our lives. No wonder it is so powerful and dominant in human life and human history."

"I never thought of it like that."

"No," he pondered, sipping his cocoa, "Most people don't. Most people are content to live an unexamined life. So sad."

"So, why is that important?"

"Because if you wish to follow the spiritual path—what Father Lawrence calls the Way of the Wilderness Warrior, then examining your life is vital, and this includes facing one's sexuality and learning to deal with it—to bring it under control, put it in its proper place, integrate it into the greater purpose of one's whole life—which is to be re-created by the workings of grace into a unique icon of Christ." His clear eyes were shining with that blend of emotion and fire that, by now, I had come to recognize as Father Aelred speaking from the heart.

"The importance of the moment of conception to the founda-
tions of personality should not, in my opinion, be underestimated.
This is what St. Augustine was getting at when he came up with
the idea of Original Sin. He wasn't the first, of course. It's there in
the psalms. 'In sin my mother conceived me,'" he quoted (51:7).
"The problem is that folks later on thought this meant that the
sexual act in itself is sinful."

"It's not?"

"Of course not. God's first commandment is for people to
have sex."

"What?"

"What was the first thing God said to Adam and Eve? 'Be fruit-
ful and multiply.' In other words, 'Get on with it. Have sex. Make
babies. When St. Augustine said we are conceived in sin, he didn't
mean sex is dirty and sinful. He'd outgrown his Manicheanism by
that point, thank God."

"Manicheanism?"

"An ancient dualistic heresy that taught that the material world—
and especially sex—was essentially sinful."

"Oh."

"Augustine was not teaching that sex is sinful but that sex had
become infected with selfishness, that it had become distorted by
idolatry."

"I don't get it."

"It's not that complicated. Very simply, because sex was so
good—so pleasurable—human beings had made it into the greatest
good, the greatest pleasure. It therefore became an idol, a substitute
for God, who should have been their greatest good and greatest
pleasure. In the ancient world, people actually worshipped sexual
pleasure. Their temples were crowded with prostitutes. Their worship included sexual orgies. Archaeologists have found statues of

gigantic phalluses that were set up as totem poles—idols for the people to worship."

"It's not so different today."

"Quite. The addiction to porn is a kind of idol worship, isn't it?"

I looked down and nodded, ashamed of myself.

"Austin." I felt as if Father Aelred were looking deeply into my heart and mind. "I do not try to remember people's confessions, and I do not speak to them about their confessions without their permission. Therefore, I wish to ask whether you would like to talk further about the confession you made the other day."

"I . . . I don't know," I stammered.

"You don't have to."

"No." I took a breath and decided. "It's okay."

"You confessed to having had relations with both girls and guys. Is that correct?"

"Yes, Father."

"Were they deep relationships? Did you love the other person?"

"No. I guess we were mostly just playing around."

"Did you have sexual intercourse with them?"

"With the girl, but not the guy."

"Why not the guy?"

"Because that's gross."

"You mean anal intercourse with another man is disgusting to you."

"Yes."

"Did you find intercourse with the girl disgusting?"

"No."

"Why was that not disgusting to you, but the other was?"

"I guess because with her it seemed natural and good. The other felt wrong."

"Why did it feel wrong? Because someone told you it was wrong?"

I thought for a moment. "Maybe, but ... no. I think it felt wrong because it *was* wrong. It was unclean. It was unnatural."

"And yet you had a desire to do this."

"Yes."

"So you have within your personality an element of homosexual desire. Do you think this is a deep desire? Is it an exclusive desire?"

"I don't know."

Father Aelred shrugged. "Maybe. Maybe not. Sometimes it is, as you say, 'just playing around.' It's a phase."

"I didn't initiate it. The other guy sort of led me into it."

"But he didn't force you?"

"No. We were drunk."

He frowned. "Don't blame the drugs."

"It wasn't drugs."

"Alcohol is a drug."

"Sorry. You're right. I can't blame the booze."

"Homosexual desire may be a thing you are passing through, but I will tell you one thing: the more you indulge that desire, the more it will become exclusive. Every sexual action we indulge in confirms and cements the particular inclination that brought us there. This is why pornography is addictive. The stimulus, once achieved, helps to confirm an inclination and cement a habit in the personality until eventually an addiction develops"

"Why do I feel this way? Why do I have this attraction to guys?"

"Good heavens!" Father Aelred said. "I don't know! From what I have read, the genesis of the homosexual condition is extremely complex. There are many theories: your mother didn't love you, so you hate women and love men. Your father didn't love you, so you love men as a way of searching for your father's love. You were a sissy at school and didn't have male friends, so you are looking for a boyfriend. You're in love with yourself, so you love other men as a form of narcissism. All these theories seem to have some validity, but, in my opinion, while they might help to answer the question of why such an inclination exists, they rarely provide a solution. The solution is the one that has been around for centuries, and it is simple common sense."

"Which is?"

"Self-knowledge and self-control. Realize that you are greater than your sexual desire. That is not your identity or your destiny. Look at it from the bigger perspective. Our sexuality is the physical and psychological aspect of our longing for love. That longing is the great human question, and the great human quest. All of us are searching for love—eternal love—and we mistake genital pleasure for the object of that search, and we see other people as the means not only to attain genital contentment but also as the object and source of love. Who that other person happens to be is secondary."

"I'm not sure I follow."

"Let me put it more simply: At the deepest level of our being, we want to love and to be loved. We are told that making love, or 'having sex,' as it's now called, is the only way to find fulfillment of the desire to love and be loved. So we are drawn by our physical urges and psychological predispositions to a particular person or type of person. We wrongly believe that genital pleasure with that person will satisfy this deeper need. However, anybody who has 'played around,' as you put it, soon realizes that having sex on its own doesn't really satisfy. It's like drugs or any other artificial shortcut to bliss. It is not really what we want. We want more than that. We want true love, which is creative, eternal, and unconditional."

"Which is impossible."

"Not really." Aelred smiled. "I have known men and women who have discovered that love—but it is always within a lifelong commitment, and it is something that is intentional, something that is constructed."

"So you're saying that love is something that is built—not something you fall into."

Aelred laughed. "Yes. It's a tower, not a pit."

"But what if two men love each other?"

"That is worthy and beautiful. That love is *phileo*—brotherhood or friendship. That's where Aelred of Rievaulx is so wise. There is nothing wrong with two men loving each other as brothers, but if they try to love each other as husband and wife, it is, as you have said, unnatural."

"They wouldn't say it's unnatural. They'd say they were born that way."

"Then they are mistaken, and in saying that, they are proving how many in our society are deeply confused about human sexuality. C. S. Lewis somewhere uses the analogy of food."

"Meaning?"

"He says food is for nutrition, but eating food is also pleasurable. But likening it to a striptease show, he asks what you would think of a restaurant where all they did was bring out plates of food and step-by-step uncovered the food to make you drool. He might have added, what would you think of a person who simply eats food for the pleasure, then vomits it up again because he doesn't want to get too full—he just wants the pleasure of eating food that tastes good?"

"That's gross."

"Indeed. Likewise, sexual intercourse is for making babies and to strengthen the love of the husband and wife. To indulge in sex merely for the pleasure is selfish and unnatural. Thus, the Church's prohibition against masturbation and pornography, prostitution, promiscuity, and every other form of sexual behavior that sidesteps love and creativity while it grabs only at self-centered pleasure. That's why I say that focusing on homosexuality—or, for that matter, any other sexual preference—is missing the point."

"Sorry, but what is the point?"

"The point is that homosexual actions—like any of the other things I just listed—are ultimately centered only in pleasure. All of these actions, homosexual or heterosexual, are by their nature inverted toward the self, not toward the other person."

"Hang on. They're giving pleasure to each other. That's not self-centered."

"If it is focused *only* on the pleasure, then it is mutually self-centered—mutually masturbatory. These relationships are, by their nature, uncreative. They either block the natural creativity through artificial contraception, or they are intrinsically uncreative because two men or two women cannot conceive a child together."

"But how does it get so twisted?"

"Concupiscence."

"What is that?"

Father Aelred rolled his eyes and sighed, "What do they teach in catechism class these days?"

"Sorry, Father."

"Not to worry," and he waved off my ignorance with a slight smile. "Concupiscence is the natural tendency we all have toward selfishness, and this is what corrupts the sexual desire. The desire for love and for sexual union is good, but it is corrupted and twisted by concupiscence."

"Can it be untwisted?"

"Only through a lifetime of hard-won self-knowledge, self-discipline, vigilance, and grace. Pope St. John Paul II said, 'Chastity is the work of a lifetime.'"

"Chastity. No sex, right?"

"Not quite. Chastity means no sex outside of marriage but also the right pursuit and practice of sex within marriage. Married people are thus also called to chastity. No sex at all is *celibacy*, which is what you are thinking of. Priests, and men and women in religious vows, are committed to celibacy. You will find some who think celibacy simply means they can't get married, but that it is okay to have sex with people. They're wrong. Celibacy means you keep your pants on, and you sleep alone."

"But why, if sex is good?"

"Celibacy is the ultimate form of self-discipline. Why do you think it is virtually universal in all religious traditions that the ones who pursue holiness are expected to be celibate? It's also the way the chains of concupiscence are broken."

"You lost me there."

"We are in bondage to concupiscence, and the chains are strongest and most profound in the area of sexuality. Therefore, when people turn off their sexual activity completely through celibacy, they eventually break the bonds of concupiscence at the foundational level of their personality, and thereby acquire enormous spiritual freedom."

"Whoa! I never thought of it like that. I guess I just sort of thought you guys had to be celibate because sex must be dirty or sinful or something."

"You and just about everyone else in the world—and unfortunately too many Catholics also understand it in this negative way."

"So where does all this fit in with Father Lawrence's Way of the Wilderness Warrior?"

"Good question. One stage of the hero's quest is the encounter with the temptress. In the classic stories, the hero comes across some sort of sexual temptation—the seductive sirens, Circe in the Greek myths, *La Belle Dame Sans Merci*."

"A Keats poem, right?"

"Yes."

"We read it in English Lit," I said. "The knight in shining armor is captivated by a bewitching woman. And Circe—she seduced Odysseus and his crew."

"And what happened to them? Do you remember?"

"They were turned into pigs."

"An apt symbol, I think. In other stories, it might simply be that the hero has a love interest. Either way, Father Lawrence would say that the great stories teach us that part of the hero's quest—part of the Way of the Wilderness Warrior—is coming to grips with our sexuality. To do so is also to deal with the Mother-Father Wound."

"The what?"

"The Mother-Father Wound. St. Augustine taught that concupiscence is a wound in the human personality. Distortions in sexuality are rooted in the circumstances of our conception, which is therefore intimately linked with our mother and father."

"I don't get it."

"Our conception should take place through the loving embrace of a man and a woman totally dedicated to each other and, ideally, within the supernatural blessing of the sacrament of Matrimony. In such a case, the child's conception occurs within the glow not only of human love but within the blessing of Divine Love. That's a good start—a great foundation for the person who will develop."

"Yeah, that sounds awesome."

"Indeed. Unfortunately, this ideal is not always the environment of a child's conception. If the sexual action takes place in the absence of love, within selfishness, or even within drunkenness or violence, the foundation of the child's whole personality is one of selfishness, abuse, addiction, or violence."

"You're saying the moment of conception itself helps to determine the person's personality and destiny?"

"It can't be proven scientifically, but there is anecdotal evidence that supports the theory, and it's logical. It makes sense, doesn't it?"

"So our parents messed us up?"

Father Aelred smiled and said, "But they didn't mean to. That's why we have to forgive them."

"One of my roommates was in counseling, and he said all the counselor wanted to talk about was his relationship with his parents. He got sick of it."

He nodded, "Yes. Psychologists have understood this problem, and they are often expert in exposing the underlying problems, but sadly, they rarely have the tools to do anything about it.

"What do you mean?"

"They talk and talk and talk about it, but they don't know what to *do* about it, except make another appointment at eighty-five dollars an hour to talk further. I knew a woman who talked to her counselor for twenty years about her mother and, at the end of the time, she still hated her mom."

"Do I have to go through that?"

"Do you want to?"

"Not really."

"Okay, then don't. However, part of your self-knowledge will be to learn about the deep influences for both good and ill that you received from your mother and father. In one way or another, to a greater or lesser extent, life will present you with this challenge. Then, as these things are revealed, you can forgive your parents and learn to honor them, as the fourth commandment tells you. This is where we differ from those who rely on only psychological counseling. We have the tools to solve the problem."

"What tools?"

"Confession, the sacraments, prayer. Through the life of prayer and by God's grace, these things are often very gently revealed to us. When people discover the resentment or even hatred they have for their parents, they can bring it to Confession and have it lifted. Also, God has given us a mother prayer and a father prayer at the foundation of our spirituality. The Hail Mary and the Our Father, when prayed at a deep, regular, and profound level, can help to reconcile and heal the Mother-Father Wound. As that is healed, there is often a deep healing of any sexual distortions that a person may be suffering from."

"So sexual problems are linked with our parents?"

"Not always, but often. The link is mysterious, and it is not necessary always to make it explicit or to understand it. The Hail Mary and the Our Father open the depth of our being to the perfect Mother, who prays for us, and the perfect Father, who created us. God knows what He's doing, and in my experience, His providence is more effective and more compassionate than psychiatric therapy."

"Do you really think that's true—that the Hail Mary and the Our Father can heal us?" I asked.

"I know it is true," Father Aelred nodded, and again, I saw his blue eyes watery with emotion, "because I have experienced it myself."

"You?" I said. "You have had sexual problems?"

"It is part of being a son of Adam and Eve," he said quietly. "It is the struggle ... to learn how to love and how to be loved."

With that, we both sat in silence. I glanced up at Father Aelred and saw him gazing into the fire, apparently lost in thought. I turned and watched it too and concentrated on its color and on its warmth.

Finally, Father Aelred heaved himself up from his chair. "Come now," he said. "This has been a serious session. Let's take a breather and hike back to the abbey. I want to hear my brothers sing Vespers and, to tell you the truth, I need some fresh air, to blow away the cobwebs in my brain."

13

The Great Ordeal

As we hiked back to the abbey, I asked Father Aelred what the next stage of the Way of the Wilderness Warrior was.

"The Great Ordeal."

"That sounds serious."

"Father Gregory—Father Lawrence's friend at St. Bede's—says the most difficult part of writing a screenplay or a novel is the long second act. In a movie, that's the hour or so that takes up the main action. It's complicated; there are unexpected plot twists and character developments. Either the audience—and the writer as he writes—are kept on the edge of their seats, or they get bored and bogged down with the long ordeal. The hero also gets bored and bogged down. The Great Ordeal is the stage of the spiritual journey that is the long second act—persevering to the end, to the final consummation and climax of the story."

We had just reached the brow of the hill, and Father Aelred said, "But let's talk about this further after dinner. Vespers first, then dinner and a short rest, and then I'll meet you in the cloister walk for a talk before Compline. How does that sound?"

"Perfect."

The cloister is a garden in the middle of the monastery surrounded by a covered walkway on all four sides. It's a place to walk slowly and meditate. To me, it was a symbol of the monk's life: enclosed by the disciplined life of prayer but open to the heavens. The cloister at Cripple Creek was a haven of silence and peace. Father Aelred was waiting for me there before Compline, and we walked around the cloister to a door on the far side. He indicated the doorway. "Here's the library. Let's duck in here rather than talk too much in the cloister."

The library had books from floor to ceiling and was dotted with long oak tables that had little reading lamps on them. Father Aelred steered me to an alcove on one side where there were a couple of armchairs.

As he settled into one and gestured to the other, he said, "Sorry I can't offer you a glass of Norcia beer!"

"Is that my Great Ordeal?" I responded.

"No indeed. In fact, part of the Great Ordeal is that it's not that great at all. It's not an exciting adventure. It turns out that the Great Ordeal is boring. It's drudgery. It's hard, tedious, seemingly thankless work to climb the mountain of perfection."

"Father Lawrence spoke about perfection. Do you think it's possible in this life?"

"Of course. The saints are evidence of it. Each saint, in his or her own way, and by reliance on grace, has achieved perfection or sanctification in this life, but one must understand that in becoming a saint, they did not become someone else. They became all that they were created to be. St. Thérèse was not someone other than Thérèse Martin—Martin was her family name—she was Thérèse Martin totally fulfilled and perfected."

"And that is the Great Ordeal?"

"Yes. The long, hard slog up the mountain. Have you ever climbed a mountain?"

"Can't say that I have."

"Well, I have. When I was a younger man, some of us monks were given a vacation in the Pyrenees—that's the mountain range that separates France and Spain. We set out to climb a mountain, and the experience taught me a lot."

"You just start at the bottom and follow the trail upward, right?"

"Not quite. The trail twists and turns, taking you upward slowly in a switchback method. This is like the liturgy. Back and forth, back and forth. The mountain trails were tiring, often monotonous and repetitious, but also exhilarating—we were out with friends, enjoying the fresh air and exercise, and emboldened that we were making the climb. And, every now and then, we'd stop to savor the view.

"Then, as we got higher, the trail became steeper and led into a rock face. The trail across the rock face was narrow and treacherous, and at times we had to leave the trail, get out our rock-climbing gear, and scale the rock face up to the next level. It was dangerous, and it required daring. Just so with the crises we come across in the spiritual life, in whatever form they manifest themselves: a personal crisis, such as the death through illness of a loved one, or perhaps a more personal spiritual crisis, an inner crisis of some sort. It takes courage and skill to navigate these passages of life, these climbs up the sheer cliff face, but, when you're rock climbing, someone always has the rope in case you fall. Even so with the life of grace. Beneath you are the Everlasting Arms."

"Did you make it to the top?" I asked.

Father Aelred smiled, and his blue eyes shone. "We did. The last part of the climb was the worst. The air was thin and, as we were above the snow line, the cold increased. I remember our fear as the sun went down and we had to pitch a tent and spend the night on the mountain. The next morning, the climb became totally open. There was no longer a clear path to follow. We had to rely only on our instincts and the sight of the peak up above that we had decided to conquer. The final ascent was across a bank of scree—loose gravel that gave way under our feet so that we slipped down and had to scramble back up—two steps forward, one step back for most of the morning, sometimes crawling on our hands and knees. Finally, we reached a ridge."

His eyes were fixed in the distance, remembering. "I thought when we reached the ridge that we had reached the summit, but, when we got there, we realized we had to stop quite suddenly. The ridge was actually the edge of a steep escarpment that dropped straight down on the other side." His hand chopped through the air. "Whoosh!"

He laughed and shook his head. "We saw that the summit was still higher off, up above us another great distance, to the right of where we stood." He waved his hand, gesturing to the right as he continued his story. "We had to hike another half mile or so along this narrow ridge, with a drop into the abyss on the left, and the steep fall of scree on the right. Our legs were wobbly by then, and I felt that, at any moment, one of us might tumble off the edge, to the right or to the left. Well, we eventually made it to the summit, and we discovered that we'd taken a wrong turn on our way up; the last half of our trek was far more treacherous than it need have been. On the far side of the summit was a clear footpath leading back down the mountainside. If we hadn't made that wrong turn, it would all have been much easier and safer."

"So that's the spiritual life, is it?"

He grinned. "Pretty much. Mostly tedious, but with some excitement and danger—especially when you choose the wrong path."

"Point taken."

"This part of the journey is sometimes called the Illuminative Stage, as you might recall from one of our earlier discussions. It is the long stage that follows an initial purification. The initial purification is the renunciation of our bodily desires, our attachment to possessions, and our former way of life. There are three renunciations that we speak of: those of the lust of the flesh, the lust of the eyes, and the pride of life. Of course, the renunciations must continue and become a way of life, but the Illuminative Stage is not one of purgation and renunciation; it is one of walking in the light and seeking not just to overcome vice but to acquire virtue. That is where it all becomes hard, tedious, and sometimes risky and dangerous work. This is climbing the mountain. Do you remember in your confession, I led you through an examination of conscience using the seven deadly sins?"

"I do."

"There are seven virtues that counter those seven vices, and acquiring the virtues is the best way to overcome the vices, just as lighting a candle is the best way to overcome the dark."

"What are the virtues?"

Father Aelred laughed. "Whole chapters and books have been written on the subject, but for starters, we can touch on them. If pride is the chief vice, it would be countered by ...?"

"Humility?"

"Correct. For homework, sit down with the *Rule of St. Benedict* and meditate on his famous seventh chapter, which discusses humility."

"Already done that."

"Well, do it again. There is more there than meets the eye on first glance."

"Gotcha."

"Next, envy. What would counter envy?"

"I don't know. Generosity?"

"Good guess, but no. Mercy. Envy is not just wanting what someone else has; it is wanting to destroy that person to get what he has. Envy manifests in hatred and ultimately violence. Mercy counters it because mercy is love's other name. Mercy is love in action. What would you say is the antidote to the next vice—wrath?"

"Forgiveness?"

"Almost. Meekness is the right answer. Meekness is not being a doormat or a mousy little creature. Meekness is a simple and humble acceptance of God's will and the free will of others. It is the ability to be and to let others be without recrimination, blame, or wrath. What about avarice, otherwise known as greed?"

"Countered by generosity."

"Yes. That's an easy one. It is more blessed to give than to grab. Lust?"

"Chastity. Got that one on the temptress thing."

He chuckled and moved ahead. "Sloth?"

"Countered by hard work?"

"The word is *diligence,* and this includes the ability and resolve to take initiatives, to man up, to step up and get things done, to stand up to evil, to fight the good fight, to get off one's backside, not only to work hard, but also to pray hard, to discipline oneself, never to give up, and to cooperate with God, knowing that with God, all things are possible. The last of the seven deadly sins is gluttony."

"Countered by fasting?"

"Temperance. You know, this is why I love our dear father St. Benedict. When you read monastic history, you realize that, in the early centuries, the monks were very hard on themselves. They seemed to have competitions in asceticism: very long fasts, living in caves for months and years until they were emaciated, sick, and smelly. Some, like St. Simeon Stylites, lived on top of a pillar in the desert. There were stories of them rolling in thorn bushes or sleeping with scorpions, in order to quell the sins of the flesh. Denying oneself is necessary, but St. Benedict steps back from extreme asceticism. He says that, in the monastery, there should be 'nothing harsh, nothing burdensome.'"

"But doesn't Jesus say in the Gospel that unless we deny ourselves, and take up the cross, we cannot be his disciples?

"Yes, but I believe Benedict understood something very important about self-denial: it is a means to an end. It is not an end in itself. Fasting, praying all night, physical self-discipline—these things are the tools to get us to the point where we love Christ more than anything else. We live the life of self-denial in order to refine our love for Christ. Benedict says it himself. The monk perseveres in his chosen life so that he gets to the point where he prefers nothing to the love of Christ. It's a positive thing, not a negative, but the negative moves us toward the positive."

"I'm not sure I get it."

Father Aelred smiled. "You will eventually. This is why Benedict seems to be so concerned about balance and temperance. He doesn't want the means to the end to become dominant. It's like the good music teacher, who knows that the student must practice, and practice hard, but also knows that it is the music that matters most, not the practice."

"Does his 'nothing harsh, nothing burdensome' apply to material possessions and to food and drink?"

"Yes. St. Benedict does not allow the monks to own any personal possessions, but he does not demand absolute poverty; in his Rule, the monastery may own property and possessions. St. Benedict expects us to not have personal property—not because possessions are sinful and not because poverty is somehow virtuous in and of itself, but because the Wilderness Warrior must acquire the attitude of detachment."

"I don't follow. I thought you had to take vows of poverty, obedience, and chastity."

"That's the Franciscans, bless them," laughed Father Aelred. "Our vows are obedience, stability, and conversion of life. Detachment is one of the ways we live out our three vows. First of all, understand that detachment is really *attachment* in the right way."

"I don't get it."

"The English poet Thomas Traherne wrote, 'Can a man be just unless he love all things according to their worth?' In other words, love everything and everyone according to its true usefulness and value. I have lots of books, but I don't value them in order to have the finest collection, the biggest collection or the most valuable first editions. That would be valuing books for their prestige, my vanity, or my superiority over others. I value the books for the information, wisdom, and entertainment within them. I may also value them for the musty smell, the comfortable appeal of being surrounded by books, and the beauty of a room full of books. This is detachment—detachment from the disordered loves and *attachment* to the rightly ordered loves, and this principle applies to all possessions and all people. It is also one of the ways we apply the virtue of temperance or balance—to love all things according to their worth."

"It connects with Aelred of Rievaulx's understanding of friendship too," I said.

"Yes. Friendship is loving the other person according to their true worth, but first of all being able to see and discern their true value."

"Which is where humility helps. If the other person is humble, it is easier to see who they really are and love them for it."

"This is why I am a Benedictine," Father Aelred said, warming to his subject, "because St. Benedict is so full of common sense. He understands people, and he understands the spiritual quest. I have to be honest. I find the other spiritual teachers too often to be prescriptive, technical, and even legalistic—as if the spiritual path must be lived out only according to these rules, that discipline, these steps, and that tried-and-true method. I'm sure they are worthy and help many, but I'm sorry. It doesn't work for me. Instead of that, St. Benedict says the monastery is 'a school for the Lord's service.' Someone has said that all he does is create the ideal environment for a soul to make progress. He knows every soul is different, but the monastery provides a hothouse for all the different seedlings to grow at their own pace and in their own way, empowered by God's grace."

I nodded. "I can see that. I thought when I came here all the guys would be like clones—or like soldiers—all in the same uniform, all indulging in groupthink, maybe sort of all brainwashed by the system, but they're not like that at all. If anything, it was my friends back at college who were all the same, conforming to the fashions and trends and all trying to fit in. The guys here are really themselves."

The bell was ringing for Compline, and I got up to go, but Father Aelred said, "If we're a little late for Compline, it will be okay. As it's Compline, just a word about prayer: it is only prayer that takes the Wilderness Warrior through the Great Ordeal."

"Father Lawrence taught us there are basically three forms of prayer: vocal prayer, meditation, and contemplation."

"Yes. That's good, and, like the three stages of the spiritual life, people often think vocal prayer is a stage you move on from—ascending to meditation and then contemplation. That's true to an extent, but most people who progress will become adept at all three, moving on to contemplation but not neglecting the other two."

At this point, Father Aelred got up and began pacing back and forth, concentrating on his thoughts. "Vocal prayer is not just talking to God and telling Him what we want. It is also the liturgy—including the Divine Office. When we sing or say the psalms and prayers, we're entering into vocal prayer—the prayer of the Church. Because this is so basic, St. Benedict takes a fair bit of time in the Rule to instruct the monks on liturgy. It is also why Benedictines have traditionally been such liturgical experts. We are prayer professionals, if you like, and the liturgy, because it is vocal prayer and the most basic prayer, is crucial."

"But doesn't it get boring? All those prayer times in the monastery?"

"You would think so, wouldn't you?" he replied. "To be sure, it does sometimes become tedious and repetitious, but that's part of the Great Ordeal, right? However, once we get into the rhythm and routine, it becomes part of life, like the mealtimes and the times for study and work. The Divine Office is a time for work and a kind of spiritual mealtime. We are nourished spiritually, but there's another aspect too. Vocal prayer uses words and our capacity for language, but the words are used to take us beyond words."

I frowned. "I'm not sure I follow."

"The words open our hearts and minds like keys to a locked door, but, once the door is open, we move into the wordless realm. From words to meditation. From words and images to the spirit and concepts beyond the words and images."

"Father Lawrence said the Rosary was the main form of meditative prayer."

"It is a good path into meditative prayer, as are all the chaplets and various rosary devotions. However, a truly Benedictine contribution to meditative prayer is Lectio Divina—Holy Reading. Did he teach you about that?"

"A little. It's reading the Bible with meditation, right?"

"The Bible and other holy books too. Holy Reading consists of four parts: Lectio—which is reading the text slowly and prayerfully;

Meditatio—meditating silently on a word or phrase from the text; *Oratio*—bringing that thought or meditation into God's presence; and *Contemplatio*—remaining in God's presence in an attitude of attention and adoration."

"So Lectio Divina actually brings people into the other two forms of prayer—meditation and contemplation."

"Correct. And the beauty of it is that the meditation and contemplation are not just letting your mind wander, nor is it indulging in the Eastern idea of contemplation—which is, as I understand it, simply a technique for making your mind a blank. Instead, your mind is dwelling on content from your reading—content that is inspired and God-given."

I stifled a yawn.

"I'm sorry," said Fr Aelred. "Is this boring?"

"No, Father. Not at all. It's just that it's been a long day."

"Probably time we went to Compline. They must have started by now. Just remember about prayer—that it is also part of the Great Ordeal. It is a long, hard climb up the mountain, but the view from the top is grand!"

The monks were singing the night office as we slipped in and sat at the back of the church. The chant swept along and over like a warm wave, and it seemed that there, in that chapel, all we had just spoken about was present and real. It lived in the high arches of the church, in the faint fragrance of incense from that morning's Mass, in the ancient Latin language, and in the young lives of my new friends, robed in black as they chanted their night psalms together.

After they sang the "Ave Regina Caelorum," there was silence in the darkened church before the monks stood and processed out in their formal pattern. Father Aelred leaned over to me and whispered, "I'm spending the night here. Too dark to go back to the hermitage."

"Do you have a room here at the monastery?"

"No, I meant I'll spend the night here in the church. I'll see you in the morning."

I woke that night at three in the morning and couldn't get back to sleep, so I grabbed my rosary and crept down to the church. There, on the carpet in front of the high altar, I saw Father Aelred prostrate with his arms stretched out. I thought he was sleeping, but then he pulled himself up slowly and knelt. He was still there after I finished my Rosary and went back to my room to get a few more hours of sleep.

14

The Belly of the Whale

The next morning, I found a note by my place at the breakfast table. It read, "Come again this afternoon. Father AL." For half a second, I wondered who Father Al was, and then laughed at myself. Aelred Looney, of course. Coffee. I needed coffee.

I checked in with the abbot about work detail for that afternoon, making sure he'd be okay if I went to the hermitage again instead, and then after lunch, I bundled up against the cold and hiked across the fields again. I was getting used to the little cabin in the valley, the chairs by the fire, and our conversations, but this time, as I pushed open the door, I discovered that the hermitage was empty. The fireplace was cold, and a draft was sweeping through the little kitchen window at the back. I called for Father Aelred, but there was no reply.

I turned back outside, closed the door, and walked around the side of the cabin where his little vegetable garden nestled at the foot of a rocky outcrop. Off to the right, halfway up the cliff, I saw a light glimmering from what looked like an alcove. There seemed to be a little path up from the garden, so I picked my way through some undergrowth at the bottom of the cliff and half hiked, half climbed up to the alcove.

I found there was a shallow cave in the rock, and Father Aelred was sitting there, legs crossed, wrapped in an old blanket, with a little brass candle lantern on the ground next to him. His beard and hair were disheveled, and his eyes were closed.

"Father? Are you all right?"

He grunted and moaned slightly; then he slowly opened his eyes, "I thought you'd be able to find me. I'm sorry I don't have the fire burning, and nothing for you to eat. I ... wasn't feeling up to it."

"Do you want to come down to the hermitage? I can get a fire going, if you like."

"No."

"Do you want me to just leave you alone? Do you need anything? Are you in trouble?"

"No, no, and no," he grumped. "I don't want you to leave me. I don't need anything, and I'm not in trouble."

"What do you want me to do?"

"If you're cold, you can have my blanket." He got up and un-wrapped the blanket, and I was surprised to see that he was not only barefoot but was clad in just a ragged pair of boxer shorts.

"I think you'd better keep the blanket," I said.

"Then if you're cold, go back to the cabin and get your own blanket. There are some in the cupboard above my bed."

So I climbed back down to the cabin, found a heavy red blanket, and climbed right back up. I sat next to him without speaking for some time, then timidly ventured, "Father. This is a bit extreme, isn't it?"

"What?"

"Sitting here in a cave in the cold in your underpants. I thought you said that St. Benedict called for nothing harsh, nothing burdensome."

"Nobody made me do this," he said. "I like it here."

"Why aren't you wearing anything?"

"Because I got hot. I was sweating. The fire was burning within me."

"Then why the blanket?"

"Because later I got cold. Shivering. Why all the questions? What is this, the Spanish Inquisition?" Then he started in on that high-pitched giggle of his. When he stopped, he looked at me with raised eyebrows and a wild look in his eyes and said, "I told you I was a bit looney. Why are you surprised?"

I grinned, "I'm not surprised. I was just a bit worried about you."

"Okay." he said. "That was nice of you. Pull up a rock to sit on. Make yourself uncomfortable."

"Here," I said, as I rolled a large stone next to him. "I'll sit on this. I just named it 'Harsh.'"

"Nice," he said. "The one I'm sitting on is called 'Burdensome.'"

There was another long silence, which, again, I finally felt compelled to break.

"Why did you ask me to come over this afternoon, if you just wanted to be alone in your cave?"

"To tell you about the next stage, of course. It's called the Belly of the Whale—and it's strange and difficult."

"Okay," I replied and waited.

After what must have been at least fifteen minutes of silence, during which 'Harsh' dug into my backside, my feet itched, and my cheeks tingled in the cold, he suddenly began speaking in what I had come to recognize as his normal and coherent pattern of speech.

"What is quite marvelous is how the spiritual journey—the Way of the Wilderness Warrior, the hero's quest, whatever you call it—is there in virtually every human culture, every religion, every myth and history and story of humanity. Of course, it takes many forms and incarnations, but the outline of the story is much the same, and the symbols and characters echo through them all and reflect one another. You know the story of the prophet Jonah?"

"Sure. He's called to go preach to some sinners, but he runs away from God on a ship until the sailors throw him overboard and he gets swallowed by a whale."

"The Bible says 'a great fish,' but go on."

"So he is in the belly of the whale for three days and then gets vomited up on the beach."

"A prefiguring of Our Lord's resurrection. He too went down into the deep darkness of the realm of death and came back on the third day."

"Oh, that's awesome!" I said. "I'd never made that connection before."

"Jesus Himself points it out when He says the unbelievers will be given the 'sign of Jonah,' and He foretells His Resurrection. They were too thick to understand it, though."

"What He was trying to say was beyond them."

"Tell me about it. Well, anyway, what is interesting to me is that many cultures have stories of people being swallowed up. Remember Pinocchio?"

"Yes! He and Geppetto are swallowed by a whale and rise again."

"Actually, in the original story by Carlo Collodi, they are swallowed by a great dogfish. Disney turned it into a whale and added the silly singing bug."

"Jiminy Cricket."

"That's right. Walt Disney killed the power of myth by making it cute. A singing insect in a top hat! Like those seven dwarves, all cute and cuddly—terrible! Tolkien got the dwarves right, with their axes and braided beards. But Pinocchio is more than cute.

If you remember the story correctly, it is after he comes back from being swallowed by the dogfish that he becomes a real boy—not just a puppet."

"That's right."

"Nice. Down into the depths to emerge as your true self. Out of the depths, your destiny."

"The sign of Jonah."

"I read once—probably in Campbell—that the Eskimos have a myth about one of their heroes who is swallowed by a whale, and the Zulus in Africa tell of a mother and her children who are swallowed by an elephant."

"And Red Riding Hood is swallowed by the wolf."

"I think it was Grandma, wasn't it?" he countered.

"Oh yeah, you're right. It was the grandmother."

"Anyway. All the stories, even back to the classical epics, echo this truth—that there must be a going down into the dark. Father Gregory, with his big thing about film, once said something along these same lines: Look how often the heroes go down into some underground place to fight their nemesis, and to also find themselves. Maybe it's the basement, maybe the subway in a city, maybe down into a cave or a well. Dark, dark, dark. They all go into the dark."

"Batman in his cave," I suggested. "Aragorn into the realm of the dead."

"It's everywhere, all this going down into the deep." Then, quite suddenly, he was quiet again, and I glanced at him, only to see him gazing out into the winter afternoon.

He said nothing for a long time, then he muttered, "It's all there in John of the Cross. Dark night of the senses. Dark night of the soul."

"I've heard of that. It was in a novel by Graham Greene, *A Burnt-Out Case*."

"I know it," said Father Aelred. "Greene was a good novelist but a bad man."

"Wasn't there a character in that book who was going through the dark night of the soul?"

"You're thinking of Ryker—a failed priest who mistakes his sinful condition for the dark night of the soul. It's laughable, really. That's what I like about Greene: his agonizing over the faith or loss of faith ends up being absurd—comical even."

"Comical?"

"Like that fellow in the Batman stories. The clown psychopath."

"You've watched Batman?"

"Read the comics when I was a kid."

"So the novel doesn't deal with the dark night of the soul?"

"Not very well, but it is accurate in portraying the fool Ryker, who thinks he is holy and is going through the dark night, when, in fact, he is locked in sin and, if I remember correctly, not only ends up murdering someone but believes himself good for doing so."

"That's right. He murders the architect at the end."

"To be precise, John of the Cross distinguishes between the dark night of the senses and the dark night of the soul, and it is not the great self-centered drama that Greene makes it out to be. Instead, it is simply this: In the first stages of the spiritual journey, the person usually enjoys the trek. Prayer is often refreshing and, as he moves into the Illuminative Stage, he feels good because he feels like he is learning to practice virtue and is making progress. When he prays, he feels like he is in touch with the Lord, and prayer helps him and comforts him."

"But I guess that doesn't last."

"Correct. St. John of the Cross talks about a dark night of the senses in which the awareness of God disappears. It is as though He has withdrawn His love for us. In this darkness, we begin to see ourselves as we really are. It feels bad, because our illusions about ourselves and about God are being shattered. We begin to see that perhaps our religiosity was not much more than an attempt to think well of ourselves, and the God we thought we loved was no more than a projection of our own emotional needs. In other words, it was a false god that needs to be destroyed, and oh, how it hurts to have our false gods broken! God does this in order to heal us, the way a doctor might break a badly healed bone in order to set it properly."

"Ouch."

"More than 'Ouch.' Agony. It's like spiritual heart surgery, complete with a saw to tear through your core. God is going way down deep in our lives to root out the lust, the greed, the pride, and the self-righteousness at the deepest level, and this work is something He does through the power of the Holy Spirit. There is little we can do to actively participate in this healing. That's why this process is called 'passive purification.'"

"What *can* you do about it?"

Father Aelred shrugged and pulled his blanket closer around him. "Not much. The experts say at that point you just have to go with the flow. Trust God and let Him get on with the work of purifying and healing. It's called the dark night of the senses because there are no spiritual or psychological feelings. God is working on you below—or perhaps above—the level of your senses. You probably won't even be aware of what He is doing. That's why the prayers seem empty, and your relationship is dry."

"Maybe it's like He puts you under a spiritual general anesthetic so He can operate."

He smiled grimly. "That's apt. I like it. Maybe extend the analogy. He's doing a heart transplant, so He has to put you under."

"Isn't there something in the Bible about that?"

"Of course!" Father Aelred exclaimed. "Ezekiel, chapter 36, verse 26. 'I will give you a new heart, and a new spirit I will put within you. I will remove the heart of stone from your flesh and give you a heart of flesh.'"

"How long does it take?"

"The process might take years. Some saints have gone through it and said they felt God was absent for a very long time."

"Why?"

"Well, I'm guessing that when God seems absent and you're not aware of His presence, that's when He can really pour out His grace because at that point, you are an empty vessel. John of the Cross said it was like a log that was on fire. The fire actually becomes one with the log as it burns it up. First, the senses and the emotions are burned up; then, in the next stage, the intellect, the will, and the memory are consumed."

"So you die."

"Spiritually, yes. The sign of Jonah. Die so you can rise again. Swallowed by the whale to be vomited out three days later. Down into the underworld to rise from the dead. Swallowed by the dogfish to return as a real boy."

"This is too deep—like, words aren't enough to really get at it."

"That's why they told stories about it. The myths, the folktales, and the Bible stories told the truth in a way that it could be experienced, even if it could not be explained."

"Father?"

"Yes?"

"Have you gone through this?"

He smiled and said, "That's the funny thing. I don't know. I've certainly had some dark days. In the monastery in France, I had a breakdown. They had me in the hospital for a couple of weeks. I guess I was broken then. I had lost everything. My family in America had disowned me, the monastic life had lost all its charm. The Lord seemed far away. My prayers fell on deaf ears. It seemed to me that there was nothing to live for—only a long, hard, lonely road ahead. But I don't know if that was just a nervous breakdown or the dark night."

"What did you do?"

"I eventually picked myself up and went back to the monastery and kept going—and that's where the liturgy and the monastic discipline keeps you going. It is there like," and he smiled at me grimly, "a rock to sit on."

"But nothing harsh."

"And nothing burdensome," he chuckled. "Seriously, the liturgy allows you to pray when you can't pray anymore. It's like surfing."

"Surfing?"

"Yes. Once you've spotted the wave, you paddle out to ride it in."

"You've been surfing?"

"Well, not recently," he smiled, "but the liturgy, like the wave, carries you to the shore."

"So you *have* gone through the dark night?"

"I didn't say that. I said I don't know, and that's part of the whole mystery and strangeness of it. God may be burning the impurities out of your life and healing you, but He's working behind the scenes. It really does feel like He is absent and doing nothing. In fact, if you do get a glimpse from time to time of the healing that is taking place, you may start to think you are making great spiritual progress, and then you'll become proud and obliterate all the good work God was doing within you. His silence is necessary."

"So what can you do?"

"I'm not sure, but the masters on this topic would say, 'Just keep doing what you're doing. Stay on track. Act like you believe even if you think you don't believe; then, when your own senses, emotions, and even your will are burned away, you're riding on grace alone.' Then, according to the theory anyway, God's will has become one with your will, and you are approaching union with Him. While this sounds blissful, they say it is more like entering into the very darkness of God, which is how we perceive the radiance of God. One mystic called it 'the Dazzling Darkness.'"

This time I was the one who chose to sit in silence for a long stretch, trying to process and absorb everything he had laid out for me. Finally I said, "I'm not sure I'm cut out for all this."

"That means you are," said Father Aelred.

"What?"

"If you thought this was something you wanted to do, then you would be proud and overconfident. The person who is called to this path refuses the call, remember?"

"Oh yeah. I remember."

"But his Refusal of the Call confirms the call because the refusal shows how seriously he takes it. Also, beneath the refusal is a far deeper attraction. He very much desires this calling, even though he is daunted by it. I suppose a bridegroom must feel like that. He desires his bride, but the responsibilities are terrifying. You are feeling this. Am I right?"

I nodded and stared into the winter afternoon, realizing that the daylight was fading.

Finally, Father Aelred got up, clutched his blanket around him, and said, "I'm ready to have that fire now. Will you build it? I'll be down soon to find us some of that hot chocolate."

"Father, it's getting dark. I'd better get back to the monastery. I'll build the fire, then head out."

"Good. You can take my flashlight that's hanging by the door. And Austin?"

"Yes, Father?"

"Don't tell anybody I was sitting up here in my shorts wrapped up in a blanket, will you?"

I smiled, "Of course not. They might think you were looney, right?"

He giggled and said, "Too right. Will you come tomorrow afternoon? I promise to be in my right mind."

"Sure. Same time?"

He nodded and sat down on his rock again. I went and built his fire, found the flashlight, and headed up the hill. I arrived back just in time for dinner.

15

The Wilderness Warrior

The next day after lunch, Abbot Leo Hendricks searched me out.
He was tall and broad shouldered, with hearty features, and overall
he looked like an Oklahoma farmer in monk's robes. He took me
aside and asked how things were going with Father Aelred.

"We're getting along just fine. He's teaching me about the Way
of the Wilderness Warrior."

Father Abbot nodded, "Ah yes, Father Gregory Morgan's ideas—
myths, movies, and mysteries. I think it's all rather eccentric and
maybe a bit gimmicky. But it has some merit, I suppose. For my
part, I prefer the Rule of Our Holy Father St. Benedict. It's more
normal—nothing eccentric or gimmicky about it."

I laughed. "The monastic life is normal?"

The abbot smiled. "Well, we think we're just about the most
normal people anywhere. It's everybody else who's crazy."

I nodded, "That's one way to look at it, and, since you mention it, I have noticed that the guys here do seem happy and, well,
ordinary. I thought they would all be weird and overly pious, but
once you see past the black robes and unusual schedules, they seem
remarkably sane. You're right. It *is* everybody else who seems crazy."

Father Abbot smiled. "Thank you for coming to visit with
us. I hope you are benefiting from your stay, and thank you for

keeping an eye on Father Aelred. You know, he and I were two of the community who went to France so long ago."

"He told me a bit about it. It sounds like a real adventure."

He chuckled. "We were young dreamers, more foolhardy than courageous."

I shrugged. "Young men are supposed to be daring, aren't they— I mean, we?"

"You were taking a risk to come here, weren't you?" he asked. "Father Lawrence told us you left college and came against your father's wishes."

"My father didn't say I *couldn't* come—just that I was a fool to do so."

"Our families thought we were fools to go to France," Father Abbot said. "And most people think Father Aelred is a holy fool living out there in that cabin."

"But the other monks love him, don't they?"

"Oh yes," the abbot said. "There is great affection for Aelred. He has become a friend to all. That's why some of us are rather concerned about him. Last winter he had a bad spell of flu, and he was very ill for a few weeks. Let me know how he's getting on, will you?"

"Of course, Father. He asked me to come over again this afternoon. Is it all right for me to go, or should I join the guys on the fence-laying team?"

"I think they've finished that round of fence laying. They're pruning the trees in the apple orchard. You can join them if you like, but I think they've got enough help there at the moment. Go down to see Father Aelred."

So, once again, I hiked across the fields and down the winding path to the hermitage. I was happy and even relieved to see smoke rising from the chimney, but, when I pushed the door open, the room was empty.

I heard his voice thickly calling me from the back right-hand corner of the cabin, behind the privacy curtain. "Austin, is that you?"

I went across to his sleeping area, pushed back the curtain, and saw him sitting up in bed under the blankets, wearing red flannel long johns.

"Father, why are you in bed?"

"Because I've come down with a nasty cold." He immediately sneezed explosively, leaving a line of dribble from his nose, which he wiped with an old blue handkerchief. He tucked it back into his sleeve.

"I'm not surprised," I said. "Sitting in that cave in your shorts. How long were you up there?"

He waved a hand as if to chase the idea away. "Oh, I don't know. Most of the day, I suppose. I was rather lost in my thoughts."

"Lost in contemplation, I guess."

He smiled weakly, "If you say so. Now, why don't you go into the kitchen and make both of us a hot toddy?"

"How do I do that?"

"A measure of whiskey in a mug to start. You'll find a bottle of Scotch under the sink. Add the juice of an orange—squeeze it fresh. You'll see the basket of oranges there. The Collins kids brought it over this morning."

"How did they know what you wanted?"

He rummaged under the covers and held up an old cell phone. "We're not completely in the Middle Ages here. I text them if I need things. Fill the mug with boiling water—that's your hot toddy—oh and add a spoon full of honey. There's a jar in the cupboard."

By the time I brought out the two mugs, Father Aelred was coughing loud and long, and when I pulled up a chair to sit by his bedside, he was gasping for breath, and his eyes were streaming.

After an eternity, and one last particularly horrible grating rasp, he spat out some vile-looking phlegm into his handkerchief. He leaned back, trembling, with his eyes closed and his chest heaving as he tried to settle.

"Oh dear!" he gasped. "Oh dear. That's not good."

I reached over to feel his forehead, as my mom used to do when I was sick. It felt hot.

"Father, you have a fever. You said yesterday that you were very hot, and then shivering cold. Shouldn't we get a doctor out here?"

"What's he going to do? Drive all the way out here just to tell me I have the flu? Tell me I should bundle up, look after myself, get plenty of fluid, and get well soon? No. I'll soldier through it. No need to worry. And Austin?"

"Yes, Father?"

"Don't tell Father Abbot I'm sick, will you? I don't want to worry him. He's got enough to worry about."

I hesitated, unsure what was the right thing to do; then finally I nodded slowly. "Okay ... but was there something you wanted to tell me, Father? Or can I get you anything else? You asked me to come over again this afternoon."

"It's the next stage. You need to hear about the next stage, and that will really send you running."

"Maybe that could wait, Father. All that coughing—maybe you should rest, not try to talk so much."

He waved off my suggestion. "Nonsense. You're here, I'm here; this is why we're here. Carpe diem, boy."

I smiled in spite of myself, resigned to the fact that there was nothing for me to do but follow his lead. "Okay," I said. "What's the next stage?"

"This is the one that it's all about. It is the stage of the Wilderness Warrior. You see, the name of this program makes it sound like something rather romantic—the Knight in Shining Armor approaching the Castle Perilous, or the Hobbits' Journey into Mordor, or Beowulf battling the Grendel beast. However, the Wilderness Warrior is not just a romantic symbol. The one who goes on this quest is indeed a warrior, and war, as the saying goes, 'is hell.' The Wilderness Warrior does do battle with dragons, and worst of all, he dwells in a wilderness. Yesterday, we discussed what the spiritual masters call the dark night of the senses—" but at this point he fell into another coughing fit and ended by gasping for breath again.

"Father, take a sip of your drink."

He spat more phlegm out, wiped his mouth, reached for his mug, and took a noisy sip. "Ah, that's better!" He smiled weakly, paused a beat, and went on. "This wilderness is even more barren than the dark night of the senses. It is called the dark night of the soul.

"At this point, the searching soul seems utterly abandoned by God. Not only is there no sense of God's presence, but a real darkness descends on the soul—a profound intellectual and spiritual darkness, so heavy that the soul, if he is not careful, can fall into despair, doubt the very existence of God, and start to believe that he is damned."

I frowned. "How can a saint believe he is damned, when he has given his whole life to love and serve God?"

"Didn't Our Lord Himself cry out on the Cross those terrible words, "*Eli, Eli, lama sabacthani*—My God, my God, why have You forsaken me?"

"Yes," I said and frowned again. "It's true. I've always wondered about that."

"Some say that He was simply quoting a psalm, and it is true that Psalm 51 has those very words, but I believe He also experienced this desolation. That is the true image of the Wilderness

Warrior—the naked, crucified man. You know, I once visited an old Franciscan monastery in Italy, where I discovered a most disturbing crucifix carved by Donatello. The figure of Our Lord hangs naked on the Cross, and of course, that was accurate. He didn't have a loincloth, as He is usually portrayed. He suffered the ultimate public humiliation. So, in that monastery, you enter a darkened room, and there it is before you—the naked Christ. Life-size and terrible. Hanging in the darkness. *Ecce homo:* 'Behold the man.' "

Aelred sat silently, except for his labored breathing, and then the coughing started again. He was trying hard to suppress the deep, lung-rattling cough but not succeeding. Eventually it burst out of him, full force again, taking over and running him through gauntlet yet again. And again, when it had subsided, he waved off any attempts of mine to help him or suggest we take a break. So instead, I turned back to the conversation of Jesus' seeming despair on the Cross.

"Did God abandon Him?"

"Some theologians argue so, but I don't believe it. I believe, in His human nature, Our Lord was convinced of that abandonment."

"And so He gives up hope."

"I didn't say He gave up hope. That would be to give in to temptation. However, He gets close to despair. He is badly tempted. Think about it. He has given everything to God, but He now feels as though God is not there. In other words, it has all been a mug's game. He has been a fool. He thought He was giving everything for the Kingdom of Heaven, but now He feels there is no such thing. He feels only the freezing cold of the cosmic darkness closing in."

"I think I understand."

"But you don't!" said Father Aelred fiercely, shaking his finger at me. "You don't understand. You still think it's a romantic adventure. It is not. It demands a condition of complete simplicity, costing not less than everything."

"And you say the saints go through this?"

"In one way or another, yes. Even dear little St. Thérèse. Did you know that on her deathbed, she admitted that if it were not for grace upholding her, she would have committed suicide?"

"No!"

Father Aelred nodded. "Yes. She went through the most terrible dark night of the soul. This is where contemplation gets you—into the desert with the wild beasts."

"So it takes courage."

"Great courage and great perseverance. But this is where the spiritual masters, like St. John of the Cross, shed some light on what is happening. They say this dark night of the soul is the purification of the memory, the intellect, and the will, just as the dark night of the senses is the purification of the emotions and the senses."

"I can see the wilderness part, but why the warrior?"

"Because this dark night of the soul does not take place in a vacuum. It is not an experience the person goes through only when he is trying to pray. It is a condition he lives in while going on with his daily life. He feels his way along in the dark while grinding on with all the demands of the outer world. Mother Teresa of Calcutta continued on with her busy life, running orphanages, traveling the world, giving speeches—all the time knowing that the world regarded her as a living saint but, within her own heart and mind, feeling that there was nothing but the void, the empty darkness."

"What's the point of it all?"

"Ah!" said Father Aelred, and then he started coughing again. As he got through it, he went on. "Good question. I think the dark night of the soul reveals, at a profound level, our humanity, our total weakness compared with God's might. Because the soul has approached the Divine Radiance, he knows, at a deep, existential level, his own darkness. The dark night of the soul is his awareness that this darkness is the darkness not of God, but of his own soul."

"What can you do about it?"

Father Aelred's eyes burned with the passion of his thoughts — or maybe they were burning with fever. "Nothing!" he said. "You can do nothing about it, except to accept that you are wandering in the wilderness as a lonely warrior, and you can't even find the dragon you are supposed to be fighting. Eliot knew it."

"Eliot?"

"T. S. Eliot. He studied the world's great spiritual writers when he was your age. The Bhagavad Gita, the Sutras—"

"The what?"

"Hindu and Buddhist Scriptures. The library records at Harvard show what books he was reading: the fourteenth-century English mystics—Dame Julian of Norwich, the *Cloud of Unknowing*, Margery Kempe—the *Imitation of Christ*. He settled on the Catholic path, thank God, and plunged into it through his own suffering, poor man."

Father Aelred leaned back on his pillow, closed his eyes, and quoted.

You may say I am repeating
Something I have said before. I shall say it again,
Shall I say it again? In order to arrive there,
To arrive where you are, to get from where you are not,
You must go by a way wherein there is no ecstasy.
In order to arrive at what you do not know
You must go by a way which is the way of ignorance.
In order to possess what you do not possess
You must go by the way of dispossession.

In order to arrive at what you are not
You must go through the way in which you are not.
And what you do not know is the only thing you know
And what you own is what you do not own
And where you are is where you are not.

"He lifted that right from John of the Cross," he finished, chuckling.

"I'm not sure I understand," I said, shaking my head.

Father Aelred put his hand on his heart and said, "Understand? Of course you don't understand. This is something one only experiences but can never explain."

"And what happens at that point?"

"At that point, you have no resources left. You are totally and utterly dependent on God, even though you are not sure He even exists. The most you may be able to do is say with all your heart, along with St. Paul, 'It is when I am weak that I am most strong'" (see 2 Cor. 12:10).

"I know you said you weren't sure if you had experienced the dark night of the soul, but do you know if you've experienced this exile of the Wilderness Warrior, Father?"

He started coughing again, and when he finally stopped, with watery eyes and a frail voice, he said, "I don't know.... I don't know. In fact, I don't think at this time that I could say that I know anything for certain." Then he smiled at me weakly and said, "So maybe that is the definition of what I am talking about, that I don't know what I'm talking about." And then he started that tiny giggle again, but it ended in more coughing and, something I hadn't heard from him before, a quiet sobbing.

Without thinking, I pulled my chair right close to his sickbed, reached over, and held him in my arms for a moment. Like a sick child, he rested his head on my shoulder, as I touched him on the forehead, smoothing his wild hair, instinctively shushing him and repeating, "It's okay, it's okay." At length, when he had quieted somewhat, I gathered my courage and tried again, "Father Father, I know you don't want me to tell the abbot, but I think you are very sick, and I should let him know."

"All right," he whispered. "All right, but not today. Come tomorrow morning after Lauds. I want to finish the last stage with you. You need to know what you're getting yourself in for.

16

A New Level of Life

I hardly slept that night, worrying about Father Aelred. It's bad to
be sick, but especially bad being sick on your own. I felt guilty for
not talking to the abbot about it, but I had promised I wouldn't.
Giving up on sleep, I got up and crept down to the church and
knelt in the darkness—just me and the red sanctuary light, burning
by the tabernacle in the distance. There in the crushing darkness,
around three o'clock in the morning, I had an experience I still
have trouble talking about.

I knew I was there to pray, but I had run out of words. I had
my rosary with me and had already prayed my way through it, but
I didn't want to go back to bed. Something was drawing me to stay
there in the dark, sitting in the back row of the great nave. Then,
as I sat there, I noticed out of the corner of my eye a movement to
my left, where a few candles were burning before the image of the
Mother of God. I turned to see what it was, and out of the shadows
stepped a monk all in black, with his cowl pulled up over his head.

He walked up the south aisle from the back of the church,
knelt before the image of the Blessed Virgin, and crossed himself.
After a few moments of prayer, he got up and lit a candle. Then
he turned and came toward me. I could see his face now, and I
realized it was Father Aelred.

He smiled and slid into the pew next to me and whispered, "Don't tell anyone about this."

"Father!" I whispered back, "What are you doing? You should be in bed."

"Shh." He said putting his finger to his lips. "I needed to talk to you. I thought you would be here. Three o'clock in the morning is the time when the veil between this world and the next is very thin."

"What does that mean?"

He looked into the distance, toward the altar and the tabernacle at the east end of the church; then he said, "Three o'clock is the hour of great temptation, when Satan and his slaves are especially busy. This is when they attack, but it is also when the angels and saints are especially available to help."

"I don't understand."

"I think you do. Why else were you wide awake and summoned to the church to pray?"

"I was worried about you," I admitted.

He sniffed, coughed a little, and patted me on the knee, "Dear boy, you don't need to worry about me. I'll be just fine."

"But you're very sick!"

"All of us are sick. Sick unto death," he whispered. "Do you remember the story of the boy Samuel?"

"I think so. He served in the temple with the old priest, and God called him in the night."

"Yes," Father Aelred said. "And he thought the old man was calling him, but finally old Eli said, 'If the Lord calls again, say, "Here I am, Lord. Your servant is listening"'" (see 1 Sam. 3:1–9).

He sat there next to me, nodding his head with his eyes closed, then he got up and went off to the south aisle, bowed profoundly to the image of the Virgin, then drifted into the shadows at the back of the church and was gone.

There in the darkness, I began to pray, "Speak, Lord, Your servant is listening." I didn't hear a voice, but, as I gazed at the altar, the red sanctuary lap next the tabernacle seemed to grow and become a blazing red light. I thought of Moses and the burning bush and found that I had kicked off my shoes without realizing it. I knelt, and unable to control myself, I started sobbing. Through my tears, I watched as the glowing tabernacle light was blurred and throbbing. After a time, I sat back in the pew, still watching the light, and drifted into a deep, silent peace.

I finally got to sleep again about an hour later and woke up suddenly, realizing the monks were concluding their morning office. As I oriented myself and watched them file out, I suddenly remembered what I had seen last night. I glanced quickly at the sanctuary lamp, and it looked entirely normal. Confused, and stiff, I hurried to brush my teeth and throw on a clean shirt before breakfast.

After eating and waking up a bit more, I made sure to catch the abbot just as he was leaving the refectory.

"Father Abbot, I need to tell you something. I think that Father Aelred is very unwell. I saw him yesterday, and he was in bed coughing and wheezing something terrible. He felt feverish, and he really looked awful. I think someone should call a doctor."

The abbot said, "He probably just has the flu again, but I'll go by the hermitage this afternoon and administer Anointing of the Sick and bring him Holy Communion. In the meantime, after Lauds, would you mind going over to sit with him?"

"He asked me to come this morning."

"Good. You go this morning, and I'll see that some of the brothers bring both of you some soup for lunch, then I'll come in the afternoon.

When I arrived at the hermitage and pushed open the door, I could hear Father Aelred hacking and gasping for breath. I pulled open the curtains and found him on the floor next to his bed. As I helped him back into bed, he managed to say, "I heard you come in. I was going to go and get you some of that hot chocolate."

"You stay put, Father," I said, "and let me get you one of those hot toddies you like."

He nodded and smiled, "That sounds better!"

I made two drinks, grabbed the folding chair, and sat by his bedside. "I have a confession to make."

"Oh, dear," he said, "not another one!"

"I couldn't wait until we were done talking. I went ahead and told Father Abbot this morning, about you being so sick."

A look of anger flashed across his face for a moment, and he said, "I asked you not to."

"I know, but I was worried. If something happens to you, and I didn't get help, I'd blame myself. Besides, Father Abbot had already asked me to let him know, before you told me not to. He wanted to know if you were okay. And, Father, your cough is very bad, and is getting worse. Can I ask ... how old are you?"

"Seventy-three, I think."

"It could be pneumonia, not just the flu. My grandfather got pneumonia, and it nearly killed him."

Father Aelred, as he so often did, dismissed my concerns with a wave of his hand. "Oh it's not pneumonia. I've got a long time left. You'll see."

"I hope so. You do seem a bit better today. Now, I have a question for you."

"Fire away."

"If you are so sick, why on earth did you get out of bed in the middle of the night last night and hike all the way to the monastery?"

"I didn't."

"But I saw you there. I was in the church praying around three in the morning, and you came and sat next to me, and you spoke with me."

"Maybe you were dreaming."

"I wasn't dreaming. I was wide awake."

"Well, I was here the whole night," he said, "here in this bed. However, I didn't sleep very well and, now that you mention it, I did have an odd dream."

"What was that?"

"I dreamt that I was with you. I was wandering in a dark place, when the Blessed Virgin came to me to help me. Then she sent me to you. I came and sat next to you."

"Then what happened?"

He laughed that little high-pitched laugh and said, "You know, I can't remember anything else about it, except that I called you by the wrong name."

"What did you call me?"

"Well, for some reason I called you Samuel. I don't know why ... I can't remember the rest. It's all very strange, isn't it?"

"Very strange," I nodded. "But you wanted me to come over this morning, so here I am. Is there more you wanted to share about the Way of the Wilderness Warrior?"

"Yes, indeed," he said eagerly. "We are at the final stage, a New Level of Life. In the classic description, it is the third stage, coming after the Purgative and the Illuminative, and they call it the Unitive Stage."

"Why Unitive?"

"Because, according to the theory, the soul has attained a state of unity with God. Jesus described it as living in Him, and Him living in us. St. John said it was 'living in love' and said, 'Those who live in love live in God and God lives in them.' " (see 1 John 4:16).

"What does that look like?"

"The person's will and God's will are infused together. Whatever the person thinks and does is thought and done within the power and love of God. Grace flows in and through the person in a way that is both natural and supernatural at the same time."

"I don't follow."

"We often think of the supernatural as being some sort of marvel or miracle that is astounding—God leaning down from Heaven and doing a kind of magic trick. Miracles are sometimes like that, but within the Unitive Stage, the soul is not just interrupted by the supernatural. The soul actually lives within the supernatural power, living a supernatural life in all things."

"Like electricity powering all the appliances in a house."

"Yes, that's a good illustration. St. Paul said it to the Galatians when he wrote, 'My life is not my own. Christ is living in me' [see Gal. 2:20]. In this stage, the person is overflowing with the fruits of the Spirit: love, joy, peace, patience, kindness, and self-control. It is like Christ is alive again. Each one becomes a unique image or icon of Christ. This is accomplished by virtue of God first pouring Himself into humanity through the Incarnation." He shifted. "Hand me that notebook on the table, will you?"

I handed him a small, red, leather-bound notebook. He opened it and read one of the notes he had scribbled there. "Listen to this," he said excitedly and then read:

> St. Cyril identified a chain by which God the Father draws and unites mortal men to His divinity. The three links in it are: first, the substantial and essential dwelling of the Father in the person of His Son by eternal generation; second, the substantial and personal dwelling of Divinity in the humanity by means of the Incarnation; and third,

the substantial and corporal dwelling of the Body of Jesus
in our bodies by means of the Holy Eucharist.[2]

He stopped reading and looked up. "This chain explains why
the mystery of liturgy is connected with the mystery of Christ and
the mystery of our divination."

"Yes, but does anybody really attain that?"

Father Aelred's eyes were glowing again, whether through fever
or excitement I wasn't sure, but he was animated as he responded,
"Yes, yes! I believe they do! I believe many, many very ordinary
Christians achieve this, by God's grace."

"I don't know any."

"You probably do, but you don't recognize them, because true
holiness does not draw attention to itself. In fact, the truly holy
simply appear to be normal because, the fact of the matter is, holiness is the full and natural condition of the human person. It is
unfortunately wickedness that seems normal to us, because there
are so many more wicked people than good people."

"But where are all these perfect people?"

"They are in the pews more than in the pulpit, I'm afraid.
They are the multitude of good, normal, devout Catholic people
who have remained faithful and who live and have lived seemingly
unremarkable lives of worship, love, and service."

"And you think they have gone through these stages — these
twelve steps of the Way of the Wilderness Warrior?"

"Not consciously, no. And to be truthful, this is why I believe
all these spiritual maps, these interior castles and stages of spiritual
growth, have only limited worth. They are helpful, to be sure, but I

---

[2] Jean-Baptiste Saint-Jure, *A Treatise on the Knowledge and Love of Our
Lord Jesus Christ.*

believe an extraordinary number of people go on this same journey and live through these same ordeals and receive these same blessings simply by following the precepts of the Church and living in a state of grace. Through the ordinary trials and tribulations of life, they go on this journey and learn to 'prefer nothing to the love of Christ,' as our Holy Father St. Benedict puts it. Through the ordinary temptations and troubles of life, they do battle in the wilderness. And do you want to know what marks them out, how to recognize them?"

"How?"

"They love the liturgy. The liturgy is a cycle of praise and worship. Their lives are centered on the liturgy, for they have understood with their hearts that the liturgy is the center and source of all things—it is where Heaven and earth meet. They love the liturgy because the liturgy is love, and it is through it that they come to be united with the source of all love—God Himself. Their love of the liturgy is marked by reverence. They do not treat the liturgy as a form of entertainment or a gathering for a pep talk for community organizers. They are reverent in their worship. And there is a second mark."

"Which is?"

"They are reverent toward other people. They do not simply love their neighbors by being nice, good, generous people. They actually treat their neighbors with reverence. You see this in our Benedictine liturgy, in which the priest, the deacon, and the altar servers bow to one another. You see? They reverence their brothers. This is a symbol of the Unitive state—reverence for God and for one another—not because they are commanded to but because they *want* to."

He had to pause for a few minutes as he was overtaken by another coughing fit. I got up to freshen his hot toddy, which he took with a smile and the barest hint of an eye roll. When he had caught his breath and let his drink start working, he picked up the thread of our conversation again.

"Did you ever go back and reread that chapter on humility from the *Rule?*"

"Yes, sir."

He closed his eyes and said, "Father Benedict puts all of this in the context of humility. To achieve true humility is to achieve this unitive state. So he says: 'Now, therefore, after ascending all these steps of humility, the monk will quickly arrive at that perfect love of God which casts out fear. Through this love, all that he once performed with dread, he will now begin to observe without effort, as though naturally, from habit, no longer out of fear of hell, but out of love for Christ, good habit and delight in virtue.' "

Then he looked at me, eyes still glowing, and said, "But there is a last line that is vital. He writes, 'All this the Lord will, by the Holy Spirit, graciously manifest in His workman now cleansed from vices and sins.' Did you hear that? He says this *is* possible, but only through grace. Did you hear him use the word 'graciously'? He is saying, just as all the masters say, 'It can be done, but God does it.' With God, with *grace*, all things are possible!"

By this time, Father Aelred was sitting upright in bed, full of passion and vigor, but his enthusiasm had exhausted him, and he quickly fell back, collapsing again into yet another fearful cough-ing fit. As this one subsided, and I tried to help him relax, as I'd done the day before, I realized just how tired he was. When his breath grew relatively quiet again, I looked down and saw that he had drifted off to sleep. I stepped back gently from his bed, but I decided I should stay close by in case he needed more help.

For a few minutes, I browsed through the books on his shelves, and then I found one of the ones he had mentioned, *The Revelations of Divine Love to Mother Julian of Norwich.* I went back and sat down next to Father Aelred's bed and spent the rest of the morning reading as he slept.

From the introduction I learned that Julian was an anchoress—a female hermit—in England in the fourteenth century. She lived in a time of great upheaval and distress, but she had visions that reassured her of God's overwhelming providence and love. She had a unitive vision of all things being contained and compressed into a hazelnut she held in the palm of her hand. It was like the final vision of St. Benedict, in which he saw the whole universe seemingly contained in a blaze of sunlight.

As I read her writings, I began to get the sense of everything I had learned coalescing, connected together in a great, coherent unity. The unitive stage was not only unity of the soul with God, but also the unity of all things in God, through God, and with God. The words from the Mass echoed in my mind, "Through him and with him and in him, O God Almighty Father, in the unity of the Holy Spirit, all glory and honor is yours forever and ever.' And I think I began to understand what Father Aelred meant when he said those in the Unitive Stage loved the liturgy, for the liturgy is the living expression of the unity and, I suspected, the primary means by which it is achieved.

At that point, he began to stir, and then Brother Matthew and Brother Nicholas arrived with some soup, bread, and cheese for lunch.

We helped Father Aelred to the table and found two more folding chairs. Over lunch, I explained to Nicholas and Matthew about the Way of the Wilderness Warrior and how it connected stories, movies, and myth to the spiritual journey.

"That is pretty awesome." Matthew was definitely interested.

"Why hasn't Abbot Leo told us about this?" Nicholas asked.

Father Aelred waved his bony hand and said, "He thinks it is all a rather silly lot of nonsense. You know him. Not an imaginative bone in his body."

The door opened, and Abbot Leo boomed, "Who hasn't got an imaginative bone in his body?"

Father Aelred looked up, grinned, and said, "Oh hello, Leo. Just in time for a bowl of soup." Then he started coughing again, so severely that he dropped his spoon and had to hold the edge of the table so as to not fall off his chair. "Oh dear," he said weakly, "I think I'd better get back to my bed."

As I helped him lie back down, I glanced at Abbot Leo, who had gone back to the door and was talking with someone just outside. After I got him settled, I went to see who it was. Abbot Leo said, "This is Dr. Hoskins. He's come to check on Aelred."

We left to give them some privacy, and, when the doctor came back out, he said, "Either he's got the flu really badly again, or this time it's pneumonia. We can't confirm pneumonia without a chest X-ray. Do you think he'd come in and submit to one?"

Abbot Leo said, "We'll get him over to the hospital this afternoon. Matthew, I'd like you and Nicholas to take Father Aelred to the hospital."

From his bed, Aelred said quietly, but still stubbornly, "Leo, I don't want to go to the hospital. Just give me the sacrament of Anointing and let me go. I'm at the end of the journey."

"Don't give up that easily, Father," said the abbot. "We've still got a lot of work to do. You're going to the hospital. You're going to have an X-ray, and you're going to receive the proper treatment."

Father Aelred shook his head, "Not going."

"Are you a man under obedience, Father?"

"Yes."

"Well, your abbot is giving you an order."

So we took Father Aelred to the hospital, and it was indeed pneumonia. They put him on a course of strong antibiotics and kept him there. A few days later, I went with Brother Matthew to visit him.

He was sitting in a chair by the window in a green hospital gown; he smiled and beckoned me over. "Matthew, would you go to the cafeteria and get me and Austin a cup of hot chocolate?"

"Sure," said Matthew.

"And Brother Matthew?"

"Yes?"

"See if they have any cookies to go with it, will you?"

"Sure thing, Father!"

"Now then, Austin," Father Aelred giggled, "did you think I was going to die?"

"It looked a close call, I'll admit it," I answered.

"It's not my time yet," he said, as he gazed out the window.

It was almost March, and some daffodils were beginning to bloom out in the hospital gardens.

Father Aelred looked back at me with his clear blue eyes, still glowing even now, and said, "Abbot Leo is right. I still have a lot of work to do. And Austin?"

"Yes, Father?"

"You have not yet begun to fight, have you?"

"No," I answered. "But I think I have at least decided to start to fight."

"Do you know that poem by Robert Frost about two roads?"

"I had to memorize it in tenth grade."

"I shall be telling this with a sigh," he said, "Somewhere ages and ages hence ..."

"Two roads diverged in a wood ... and I ... " I quoted.

"I took the one less traveled," he said.

"And that has made all the difference," we said together.

Epilogue

I stayed at Cripple Creek for the rest of the semester. When the rest of our class graduated in May, I traveled back to Charleston for the retreat at Hilton Head that Father Lawrence had promised all of us.

The retreat house was a large conference center, right on the beach. We all arrived, found our rooms, unpacked, and turned up for dinner in the dining room.

Michael came in, slapped me on the back, and said it was good to see me. Jordan was joking with Catherine, and JohnMark and Jenny arrived together. Shelby looked nervous but happy to see us. She asked where Clarke was.

Father Lawrence said, "Clarke can't make it."

Charlie sat down with his plate from the buffet and joked, "Where's Flo? I could use a plate of her spaghetti."

Father Lawrence said a blessing, and we all started in with our meals and with our news. I was feeling great after my time at Cripple Creek but was eager to hear what sort of adventures my eight friends had been through.

After dinner, we went into the lounge, directed by Father Lawrence. He waited as we all got ourselves settled.

"Six months ago," he began, "I set a challenge for each of you—a simple challenge to go and meet someone who would be a mentor for you on your own spiritual journey. So tell us. What happened? Just the short version, please. Who wants to go first?"

"I will," I said. "My mentor was an odd but wonderful old monk who lives in a cabin in Oklahoma. He took me through the various stages of the Way of the Wilderness Warrior, and I also learned a lot about Benedictine monks and monasteries. I had a terrific time."

Michael was sitting next to me, and I looked at him as I finished. He smiled and jumped in, "I met a professor of philosophy who showed me how the spiritual quest connects with all the great philosophical and theological systems. He set a course of study for me, and he wants me to finish my degree here and apply for grad school."

"Charlie?" Father Lawrence asked

"My guy was a Marine chaplain. He connected me with military history—turns out some of the greatest soldiers were also Wilderness Warriors. He wants me to finish my degree and thinks I should sign up for seminary and follow in his footsteps as a military chaplain."

"And will you?" Jenny asked.

Charlie shrugged, "I don't know yet. The Marines, probably. Chaplain and priest? I'm not so sure."

"What about you, Jenny?"

Jenny rolled her eyes, "I'm sorry, Father, but you sent me to Nashville, Tennessee, to meet with Sister Anna Grace."

"That's right." Father Lawrence grinned. "What happened?"

"She said the best thing for me to do was to join one of their vocation weekends, and she'd take it from there."

"So did you?" Catherine asked.

"Yes, and by then I was feeling guilty, like I was supposed to be one of those Dominican sisters, so I listened and joined in the retreat with a bunch of other girls, but then this other nun sat down with me and I told her how I felt I had to be there, and she laughed and told me I definitely did not have a vocation, and I shouldn't worry about it."

"But what did Sister Anna Grace say?" Father Lawrence asked.

"Because going on a vocations retreat wasn't really the idea."

"She said the vocation retreat was kind of a test."

"And then?" Shelby asked.

"I got mad and said I didn't want to stay there anymore. I'm sorry, Father—it really wasn't for me."

"So, what did you do next?" Father Lawrence asked.

"She came over to Ireland to see me!" JohnMark jumped in. "You sent me to this Irish priest in a seminary, and he told me about the different stages of the Wilderness Warrior and suggested that I should live them out as a priest, but, to tell you the truth, Father, Ireland in the winter is a bit damp and drafty. I stuck it out with the seminarians for a few weeks and had some more meetings with Father O'Donnell. But when Jenny showed up unexpectedly, I decided to use some of the money I'd saved up, and we traveled to Spain together and hiked the Camino."

Jenny said, "As we went, JohnMark told me all about the different stages of the journey, and it was amazing how they matched up with what we were going through on the Camino."

Charlie chimed in, "It was kind of the same when I got talking to the guys at the base who had gone through basic training. The stages of the journey made sense because they had gone through so much of it: leaving the Ordinary World, Hearing the Call, Refusing the Call, and so forth."

"Jordan?" Father Lawrence asked.

"I went to New York," Jordan responded, "and found Father Vincent, who is the prior of the Franciscan Friars of the Renewal.

They are a bunch of really cool young monks who live and work in the inner city."

"Friars," I interrupted. "Friars work in the world. Monks are enclosed in a monastery."

"Sorry!" Jordan replied and laughed and shook his head. "I'm not so hot on the technicalities. Anyway, Father Vincent gave me a place on their novice program—just an informal place, and I worked in their homeless shelter in between sit-downs with him, when we talked me through the stages, like the rest of you guys did."

"Are you going back?" Father Lawrence asked.

"Me?" Jordan replied, "I don't think so, Father. I liked being there, and Father Vincent was awesome, but it's not the life for me. But I'm glad I went. I learned a lot, and whatever life throws at me, the different stages are going to help."

Shelby said, "I went to New York too. Sister Gemma is this super-sweet Indian nun who's part of the Missionaries of Charity. They work in New York with single moms who have troubles like drug addiction or prostitution. I lived with the sisters, and Sister Gemma walked me through the stages. By the way, Father, she thinks you're fantastic."

Jenny said, "I think that's awesome. Are you going to be a Missionary of Charity sister, Shelby?"

"I'm thinking about it. Maybe."

"Catherine, how was England?" asked Father Lawrence.

"England was just lovely," said Catherine. "I had a wonderful time. St. Cecilia's Abbey is on the Isle of Wight, which is this smallish island off the coast of England. Dame Etheldreda is a Benedictine nun. She's also a musician and composer. She writes liturgical music. She took me through the stage of the Wilderness Warrior, and she wants me to go back and join them as a postulant."

"What's that?" Jenny asked.

"It's the first stage of becoming a Benedictine nun. After that, you become a novice for a year or two, then you can take simple vows, which are for five years. After that, you take solemn vows, which are for life."

"Are you going to do it?" Shelby asked.

"I don't think so," said Catherine.

"Why not?"

"Well," Catherine said, blushing, "While I was there, Clarke came to visit. He also went to New York, you know, and his mentor was an executive in a stockbroker's firm."

"Wow!" said Jordan, "Father Lawrence, you really are connected."

"Let's hear Catherine out," Father Lawrence said solemnly.

"So Clarke just turned up," she turned to Jenny, "I guess like you just turned up in Ireland to see JohnMark."

Jenny said, "Okay. So what did you do about it?"

"Clarke was really upset when he came to see me. He said the stockbroker thing really threw him. He realized he wasn't cut out for that, even though the mentor guy he went to see tried to explain that it was possible to live out the twelve stages in the world of finance. Clarke said that despite all that reassurance, the financial world just seemed too cutthroat and stressful. So he ran away, and came to find me. He said ... well," and she finished in a rush, "he said he loved me and wanted to marry me."

"You're kidding me!" cried Jenny. "Clarke?"

"So what did you do?" asked Shelby.

"I wasn't ready for that, so I told him to cool off and go to Quarr Abbey. I had met one of the monks from Quarr—Father Mark."

"Hang on," Jordan said. "What's Quarr Abbey?"

I answered, "It's a Benedictine Abbey in the same congregation as Cripple Creek, but it's also there on the Isle of Wight, like the convent. So, Catherine, what happened to Clarke?"

"He really liked Father Mark, who, as it turned out, knew about the twelve stages from Dame Etheldreda. He's a writer and a poet, so he kind of connected with all the literary stuff. Anyway, he spent some time with Clarke."

"Where's Clarke now?" Charlie asked.

Catherine said, "He's still at Quarr."

"Clarke is a novice monk," Father Lawrence said. "He decided to stay."

"Oh wow!" I said. The news completely blew me away. Clarke was the last one I would have expected to commit to the religious life, and when I heard about Clarke's decision, I spoke up, "That does it," I said. I gulped, and went on, "Something else happened to me at Cripple Creek." And then I told my friends about the night visit of Father Aelred in the abbey church.

"What?" said Jordan. "Do you think he was bilocating?"

"What's that?" Jenny asked.

So I explained about bilocation, and JohnMark joined in and told a couple of the stories about Padre Pio.

Catherine whispered, "That's amazing, and, Austin, you think this monk—Father Whatshisname …"

"Aelred Looney."

"You think Father Looney was bilocating?"

"I don't know what else to think," I said. "The next day he said he was sure he didn't leave his cabin."

"What else happened?" Father Lawrence asked.

"After he left, I sat in the darkness, and the sanctuary light seemed to grow and be a blazing fire."

"Like the burning bush," JohnMark said, "calling you."

"You started seeing things," Jenny sneered.

"Well, maybe I did, Jenny! I mean, maybe I did see things clearly for the first time!—and I'm not ashamed of that." I realized I had started tearing up, and I sniffed as subtly as I could and wiped my eyes.

Catherine said quietly, "I understand, Austin. I understand."

"And what are you going to do about it?" Father Lawrence asked.

I pulled myself together and blurted out, "Well, I'm sure not going to be outdone by Clarke. I'm going to finish my degree and graduate at Christmas, then I'm heading back to Oklahoma."

Father Lawrence was grinning, "Go for it!"

"Isn't it cold there in the winter?" Jordan asked.

"I like the cold," I said.

"I'm sorry," Jenny said. "I'm happy for you, and I can see visiting and learning about this stuff, but giving your whole life to it? Isn't it, you know, a bit of a wasted life? At least the nuns I went to see were teachers. You know. They were doing something useful. Hiding yourself away. It's just not normal."

"I think it's the most normal thing in the world." And I smiled, remembering my conversations at Cripple Creek. "It's the rest of the world that's one big nuthouse."

"That life is pretty hard," JohnMark said.

"There's nothing harsh about it," I answered, nodding to Father Lawrence.

He nodded back, thought for a moment, and replied with a smile, "And nothing burdensome."

Let us run on the path of God's commandments, our hearts overflowing with the inexpressible delight of love.

—*The Rule of St. Benedict*

Bibliography

Aelred of Rievaulx. *Spiritual Friendship*. Translated from the Latin by Laurence Graceland. Collegeville, MN: Liturgical Press, 2010.

Bell, Luke, O.S.B. *A Deep and Subtle Joy: Life at Quarr Abbey*. Mahwah, NJ: Hidden Spring, 2006.

Burke, Daniel. *Navigating the Interior Life: Spiritual Direction and the Journey to God*. Steubenville, OH: Emmaus Road, 2012.

Campbell, Joseph. *The Hero with a Thousand Faces*. London: Fontana, 1993.

Cassian, John. *Conferences*. Translated from the Latin by Colm Luibheid. Mahwah, NJ: Paulist Press, 1985.

Dundes, Alan, ed. *Sacred Narrative: Readings in Theory of Myth*. Berkeley: University of California Press, 1984.

Fagerberg, David. *Liturgical Dogmatics: How Catholic Beliefs Flow from Liturgical Prayer*. San Francisco: Ignatius Press, 2021.

Feiss, Hugh, O.S.B. *Essential Monastic Wisdom*. San Francisco: Harper, 1999.

Garrigou-Lagrange, Réginald, O.P. *The Three Ages of the Interior Life*. Translated from the French by Timothea Doyle. New York: Herder Books, 1948.

Koenemann, Cassian, O.S.B. *The Grace of Nothingness: Navigating the Spiritual Life with Blessed Columba Marmion.* New York: Angelico Press, 2022.

Levi, Peter. *Frontiers of Paradise: A Study of Monks and Monasteries.* London: Collins Harvill 1987.

Martin, Ralph. *The Fulfillment of All Desire.* Steubenville, OH: Emmaus Road, 2006.

Merton, Thomas. *The Seven Storey Mountain.* London: Society for Promoting Christian Knowledge, 1990.

Moorhouse, Geoffrey. *Sun Dancing: A Medieval Vision.* London: Weidenfeld and Nicholson, 1997.

Norris, Kathleen. *The Cloister Walk.* Oxford: Lion Publishing 1996.

Nouwen, Henri J. M. *The Genesee Diary: Report from a Trappist Monastery.* London: Darton, Longman and Todd, 1976.

Pitre, Brant. *Introduction to the Spiritual Life.* New York: Image Books 2021.

Paine, Scott Randall. *The Other World We Live In.* New York: Angelico Press, 2021.

Segal, Robert, ed. *In Quest of the Hero.* Princeton, NJ: Princeton University Press, 1990.

Slough, Mary Dominique. *The Life and Teaching of Pachomius.* Leominster, UK: Gracewing, 1998.

Wetta, Augustine J., O.S.B. *Humility Rules: St. Benedict's Twelve-Step Guide to Genuine Self-Esteem.* San Francisco: Ignatius Press, 2017.

About the Author

Father Dwight Longenecker was brought up in an Evangelical home in Pennsylvania and studied English and speech at Bob Jones University before being trained for ministry in the Church of England at Oxford. He served for fifteen years as an Anglican priest before he and his family were received into the Catholic Church.

In 2006, Father Longenecker returned to the United States to be ordained a Catholic priest under the pastoral provision for married former Protestant ministers. He now serves as the pastor of Our Lady of the Rosary parish in Greenville, South Carolina, and is an oblate of Belmont Abbey. He is married to Alison, and they have four grown children.

Father Longenecker is the author of more than twenty books on Catholic Faith and culture. His blog, *Standing on My Head*, is one of the most widely read Catholic blogs. Father Longenecker also contributes to a wide range of magazines, journals, websites, and podcasts. You can follow his writings, listen to his podcasts, join his online courses, browse his books, and be in touch at DwightLongenecker.com.

Sophia Institute

Sophia Institute is a nonprofit institution that seeks to nurture the spiritual, moral, and cultural life of souls and to spread the gospel of Christ in conformity with the authentic teachings of the Roman Catholic Church.

Sophia Institute Press fulfills this mission by offering translations, reprints, and new publications that afford readers a rich source of the enduring wisdom of mankind.

Sophia Institute also operates the popular online resource CatholicExchange.com. *Catholic Exchange* provides world news from a Catholic perspective as well as daily devotionals and articles that will help readers to grow in holiness and live a life consistent with the teachings of the Church.

In 2013, Sophia Institute launched Sophia Institute for Teachers to renew and rebuild Catholic culture through service to Catholic education. With the goal of nurturing the spiritual, moral, and cultural life of souls, and an abiding respect for the role and work of teachers, we strive to provide materials and programs that are at once enlightening to the mind and ennobling to the heart; faithful and complete, as well as useful and practical.

Sophia Institute gratefully recognizes the Solidarity Association for preserving and encouraging the growth of our apostolate over the course of many years. Without their generous and timely support, this book would not be in your hands.

www.SophiaInstitute.com
www.CatholicExchange.com
www.SophiaInstituteforTeachers.org